PERFECTING THE U.S. CONSTITUTION

ANTHEM STUDIES IN LAW REFORM

Anthem Studies in Law Reform bridges the gap between legal activism and academic scholarship by publishing short books (20,000 - 30,000 words) focused on law reform. Each title explores why and how a particular area of law needs to be reformed. Covering all areas of law and all jurisdictions, books in the series are written in an authoritative yet accessible style which will engage academics, practitioners and upper level students. This series publishes short monographs, edited collections, handbooks, companions and textbooks. These books are published in paperback and ebook formats, at affordable prices.

Series Editor
Russell Sandberg – Cardiff University, UK

Editorial Board
Thom Brooks – Durham University, UK
Faith Gordon – Australia National University, Australia
Jane Mair – University of Glasgow, UK
Mitchell Travis – University of Leeds, UK

PERFECTING THE U.S. CONSTITUTION

27 AND COUNTING, THE AMENDMENTS THAT SHAPED AMERICA'S FUTURE

BLAINE KALTMAN

ANTHEM PRESS

Anthem Press
An imprint of Wimbledon Publishing Company
www.anthempress.com

This edition first published in UK and USA 2026
by ANTHEM PRESS
75–76 Blackfriars Road, London SE1 8HA, UK
or PO Box 9779, London SW19 7ZG, UK
and
244 Madison Ave #116, New York, NY 10016, USA

© 2026 Blaine Kaltman

The author asserts the moral right to be identified as the author of this work.

All rights reserved. Without limiting the rights under copyright reserved above,
no part of this publication may be reproduced, stored or introduced into
a retrieval system, or transmitted, in any form or by any means
(electronic, mechanical, photocopying, recording or otherwise),
without the prior written permission of both the copyright
owner and the above publisher of this book.

British Library Cataloguing-in-Publication Data
A catalogue record for this book is available from the British Library.

Library of Congress Cataloging-in-Publication Data: 2025936859
A catalog record for this book has been requested.

ISBN-13: 978-1-83999-633-7 (Hbk) / 978-1-83999-634-4 (Pbk)
ISBN-10: 1-83999-633-1 (Hbk) / 1-83999-634-X (Pbk)

This title is also available as an eBook.

For Mom and Shujie

CONTENTS

Acknowledgments ix
About the Author xi
Introduction xiii

THE BILL OF RIGHTS   1

CHAPTER 1   Fundamental Rights:
The First Amendment   3

CHAPTER 2   Bearing Arms: The Second Amendment   19

CHAPTER 3   Innocent until Proven Guilty: The
Third through Eighth Amendments   29

CHAPTER 4   This and No More: The Ninth and
Tenth Amendments   91

AMENDMENTS ELEVEN TO TWENTY-SEVEN   105

CHAPTER 5   What Federal Courts Cannot Do:
The Eleventh Amendment   107

CHAPTER 6   The President and Vice President:
The Twelfth, Twentieth, Twenty-Second,
and Twenty-Fifth Amendments   111

CHAPTER 7	The Civil War and Reconstruction, Slavery to Civil Rights: The Thirteenth, Fourteenth, Fifteenth, and Twenty-Fourth Amendments	127
CHAPTER 8	Money Makes the World Go Round: The Sixteenth, Seventeenth, and Twenty-Seventh Amendments	159
CHAPTER 9	To Drink or Not to Drink, that is the Question: The Eighteenth and Twenty-First Amendments	169
CHAPTER 10	New Voters: The Nineteenth, Twenty-Third, and Twenty-Sixth Amendments	177

Afterword: Looking Back and Going Forward   189

ACKNOWLEDGMENTS

This book is dedicated to my parents, who inspired me to write it, and who made valuable suggestions that greatly improved the text.

My father, Al Kaltman, is the greatest man I've ever known, a living example of the American dream. He taught me to love our country through its history, and also to serve it. The brave men and women I worked with as a U.S. State Department Foreign Service Officer, members of the military, diplomatic core, and intelligence community, have my deepest respect and gratitude for their service.

Gwen Snyder Kaltman, my brilliant mother, taught me how to write, and the power of a good story told well. Her unquenchable intellectual curiosity is a constant inspiration to me. I would also like to thank my partner and soulmate, Shujie Wang, who has always encouraged me not to just chase dreams, but rather to catch them.

Golda Merline and the team at Anthem deserve my thanks for bringing this project to fruition.

Finally, I am compelled to acknowledge James Madison and the Framers of the Constitution. Never before in history had such an amazing assemblage of political thinkers come together to create a document of such profound and lasting impact. The United States, indeed the entire world, owes them a debt that could never truly be repaid.

ABOUT THE AUTHOR

Blaine Kaltman is a former United States Department of State Foreign Service Officer. He is the recipient of two Department of State Meritorious Honor Awards. He holds a doctorate in sociology from the University of Queensland in Brisbane, Australia. He is fluent in Mandarin Chinese. He is the author of *Under the Heel of the Dragon: Islam, Racism, Crime, and the Uighur in China.* He currently teaches American Government and sociology at Yorktown High School in Arlington, Virginia.

INTRODUCTION

We the People of the United States, in Order to form a more perfect Union, establish Justice, insure domestic Tranquility, provide for the common defence, promote the general Welfare, and secure the Blessings of Liberty to ourselves and our Posterity, do ordain and establish this Constitution for the United States of America.
      —**Preamble to the United States Constitution**

The debt we owe to the brilliant men who drafted the Constitution is incalculable. Recognizing that, with the passage of time, their document would likely require modifications, the Framers included provisions for amending the Constitution. The twenty-seven amendments that have been ratified to date have played a pivotal role in the continuing effort to perfect our Constitution.

This book looks at U.S. history and the American experience through the lens of the Constitutional Amendments. It discusses why each Amendment was adopted, the importance of each Amendment, how the Amendments have been interpreted, and the impact they have had on American society.

The Amendments have shaped and continue to shape the development of our nation. They guarantee the fundamental rights and liberties that Americans enjoy. They tell America's story from the abolition of slavery to women's suffrage, and to granting young men and women who are old enough to fight and even die for their country, the right to vote.

The Amendments play a vital role in the quest for gender and racial equity, and the continuing struggle to achieve social justice. The story of the Amendments includes America's dalliance with abstinence, the fourteen years of prohibition. They detail the changes in presidential elections, succession, and term limits, the direct election of senators, and the imposition of a Federal income tax.

The Amendments are the result of the American people's continuing efforts to perfect our Constitution, first through Acts of Congress, then through ratifications by State Legislatures, and finally by judicial review and interpretation.

Amending the Constitution

It is not easy to amend the Constitution. Nearly 12,000 amendments have been proposed, but only 27 have become law. Article V of the Constitution states that

> The Congress, whenever two thirds of both houses shall deem it necessary, shall propose amendments to this Constitution, or, on the application of the legislatures of two thirds of the several states, shall call a convention for proposing amendments, which, in either case, shall be valid to all intents and purposes, as part of this Constitution, when ratified by the legislatures of three fourths of the several states, or by conventions in three fourths.

To-date, none of the amendments have been proposed by a Constitutional Convention. They were all passed by a two-thirds majority in both the House and the Senate, and then ratified by three-quarters of the State Legislatures. Today, 288 House members and 67 Senators would have to vote for a proposed amendment, which would then need to be ratified by 38 states before it could become law.

Several suggestions have been made to change the process by which the Constitution is amended. Sarah Isgur, an author at *The Dispatch*, has proposed lowering the threshold from passage by two-thirds vote in both the House and the Senate to passage by a simple majority, with ratification not by three-quarters of the states but by two-thirds (34) of them.

Stephen E. Sachs, the Antonin Scalia Professor of Law at Harvard Law School, has suggested inverting the amendment process by first having a proposed amendment ratified by three-quarters of the state legislatures and then sent to Congress for passage by a two-thirds majority vote in both the House and the Senate.

Ethan Herenstein, a staff attorney in the ACLU (American Civil Liberties Union) Voting Rights Project, has proposed allowing voters to use ballot initiatives to call for a constitutional convention, propose amendments to the Constitution and even block State Legislatures from ratifying unpopular amendments.

The proposals to make it easier to amend the Constitution stem from the premise that the American political process has become so polarized and dysfunctional that significant positive change can only be achieved by amending the Constitution.

The final chapter of this book discusses amendments that were sent to the states for ratification, but were not ratified. It also addresses the contentious issues surrounding the imposition of a deadline by which a proposed amendment must be ratified, and whether a state legislature having once ratified a proposed amendment can withdraw its ratification. Finally, it looks at amendments that have been proposed by individuals who passionately feel that only by their passage can we perfect our Constitution.

THE BILL OF RIGHTS

The Constitution that was sent to the states for ratification did not contain a Bill of Rights even though the matter had been the subject of heated debate among delegates to the Constitutional Convention. Congress met for the first time on March 4, 1789, and the adoption of a Bill of Rights was its first order of business. Seven months later, on September 25, 1789, Congress approved and sent to the states for ratification twelve amendments that had been drafted by James Madison. Ten of these were ratified by three-fourths of the state legislatures, and on December 15, 1791, they were added to America's foundational document, the Constitution, and became the law of the land.

The ten amendments added to the Constitution contain specific guarantees of personal freedoms and rights, clear limitations on the government's power in judicial and other proceedings, and explicit declarations that all powers not specifically granted to Congress by the Constitution are reserved for the states or the people. These first ten amendments are commonly referred to as The Bill of Rights.

CHAPTER 1

FUNDAMENTAL RIGHTS: THE FIRST AMENDMENT

The First Amendment guarantees freedom of religion, speech, the press, assembly, and petition. It reads:

> Congress shall make no law respecting an establishment of religion, or prohibiting the free exercise thereof; or abridging the freedom of speech, or of the press; or the right of the people peaceably to assemble, and to petition the Government for a redress of grievances.

RAPPS is an easy way to remember these freedoms: Religion, Assembly, Petition, Press, Speech.

Religion

Let's start with Religion. The R in RAPPS. When asked, "Do you believe in God," 81% of Americans polled by Gallup in 2022 responded "Yes." Just as the United States is a melting pot of different ethnic, racial, and cultural backgrounds, America is also home to a diverse array of religious beliefs. The First Amendment prohibits Congress from establishing a religion, and from prohibiting the free exercise of one.

But what about prayer in public schools? Saying a prayer, and even reading a section from the Bible, along with the Pledge of Allegiance, was common in U.S. public schools halfway through the twentieth century.

In New York, the State Board of Regents had written a nondenominational prayer that was to be recited along with the Pledge of Allegiance at the start of the school day. Students were allowed to not participate in the prayer. If they didn't want to pray, they could just sit quietly. But not participating in morning prayer could bring unwanted attention, and even ridicule from other students. In 1962, a student's parents sued the Board arguing that having officially sponsored prayer in school, even if you don't have to participate, was unconstitutional. Why? Because, they believed it violated what's known as the Establishment Clause of the First Amendment. This part: "Congress shall make no law respecting an establishment of religion, or prohibiting the free exercise thereof."

The suit ended up in front of the Supreme Court in a case known as *Engel v Vitale*. The Supreme Court sided with the student's parents, and since then has repeatedly ruled that school-mandated prayers in public schools are unconstitutional. Public schools are part of the government, and the government "shall make no law respecting an establishment of religion."

Summarizing the majority opinion of the Supreme Court in this landmark case, Justice Hugo Black wrote: "We think that by using its public school system to encourage recitation of the Regents' prayer, the State of New York has adopted a practice wholly inconsistent with the Establishment Clause ... It is no part of the business of government to compose official prayers for any group of the American people to recite as a part of a religious program carried on by government." The dissenting opinion, written by Justice Potter Stewart, argued that no "official religion" was established by permitting those who wanted to say a prayer to say it. And, therefore, having prayer in a public school was constitutional.

In 1976, President Jimmy Carter, a Democrat, and a prominent Baptist layman, expressed his opposition to "the government mandating a prayer in school." While his successor, President Ronald Reagan, favored "a constitutional amendment to permit voluntary school prayer."

Former Speaker of the House of Representatives, Newt Gingrich, wrote this proposed school prayer amendment: "Nothing in this

Constitution shall be construed to prohibit individual or group prayer in public schools or other public institutions. No person shall be required by the United States or by any State to participate in prayer. Neither the United States or any State shall compose the words of any prayer to be said in public schools." However, his amendment never got very far.

The argument for prayer in public schools is that school prayer develops moral character. Proponents believe that schools must do more than train children's minds academically. They must also nurture their souls and reinforce good values. Those in favor of prayer in public school also contend that we have seen an increase in gun violence, alcohol and drug use, and teen pregnancy since prayer was taken out of the classroom.

Of course, from a scientific standpoint, this argument is specious. Did those behaviors increase because we stopped praying in school, or because a lot has changed since 1962? Today, virtually everyone has a cell phone and access to the Internet with its wide array of personal communication and social media platforms. In 1962, no one was texting or posting on Facebook or TikTok. There were no video games like Mortal Kombat, Grand Theft Auto, or Soldier of Fortune. Amazon Prime, HBO, Netflix, and other streaming services did not exist, and Americans were watching shows like The Beverly Hillbillies and Little House on the Prairie instead of Game of Thrones and Euphoria. Since 1962, Americans have started dressing more casually, comic book movies have become ubiquitous, and we started drinking boutique café lattes and energy drinks. One could also argue that these are reasons for a seeming moral decline in society.

The argument against prayer in school is that public schools exist to educate, not to proselytize. Children in public schools are a captive audience. Therefore, making prayer an official part of the school day is coercive and invasive. Religion is private, and schools are public, so it is appropriate that the two should not mix. Furthermore, to introduce religion in our public schools builds walls between children who may not have been aware of religious differences before, and may single out students with different religious views.

So-called moment of silence laws have to-date been deemed Constitutional. Virginia's moment of silence law, for example, mandates "the daily observance of one minute of silence in each classroom ... During such one-minute period of silence, the teacher responsible for each classroom shall take care that all pupils remain seated and silent and make no distracting display to the end that each pupil may, in the exercise of his or her individual choice, meditate, pray, or engage in any other silent activity which does not interfere with, distract, or impede other pupils in the like exercise of individual choice."

In *Kennedy v the Bremerton School District* (2022), the Supreme Court, in a 6-3 decision, ruled that the Bremerton School District had violated the First Amendment rights of Joseph A. Kennedy, an assistant football coach at Bremerton High School, when it refused to renew his contract. After each football game, Kennedy would kneel at the fifty-yard line and quietly pray. In the majority opinion, Justice Neil Gorsuch wrote:

> Respect for religious expressions is indispensable to life in a free and diverse Republic—whether those expressions take place in a sanctuary or on a field, and whether they manifest through the spoken word or a bowed head. Here, a government entity sought to punish an individual for engaging in a brief, quiet, personal religious observance doubly protected by the Free Exercise and Free Speech Clauses of the First Amendment. And the only meaningful justification the government offered for its reprisal rested on a mistaken view that it had a duty to ferret out and suppress religious observances even as it allows comparable secular speech. The Constitution neither mandates nor tolerates that kind of discrimination.

In her dissent, Justice Sonia Sotomayor wrote that the Court's decision was misguided because

> It elevates one individual's interest in personal religious exercise, in the exact time and place of that individual's choosing, over

society's interest in protecting the separation between church and state, eroding the protections for religious liberty for all.

Assembly

Moving on to the A in RAPPS. The right to assemble: "Congress shall make no law ... abridging ... the right of the people peaceably to assemble."

In 1970, Dennis Coates and four other individuals were arrested in Cincinnati, Ohio, for violating a city ordinance that made it illegal for three or more individuals to assemble in a public place and "there conduct themselves in a manner annoying to persons passing by, or to occupants of adjacent buildings." Coates appealed his conviction, and the Supreme Court ruled in his favor. Justice Potter Stewart wrote, "In our opinion, this ordinance is unconstitutionally vague because it subjects the exercise of the right of assembly to an unascertainable standard, and unconstitutionally broad because it authorizes the punishment of constitutionally protected conduct."

The right to assemble gives everyone the freedom to freely associate with one another in public in support of a common cause or shared value. Which means we can march together. But it also means we can have barbecues, game nights, parties, and large gatherings in restaurants. The freedom to meet in groups is something we all just take for granted but imagine if we didn't have that right.

Tibetans who meet in groups deemed too large by the Chinese Government are beaten and often imprisoned, because the Chinese Government fears the right to assemble will lead to another one of our most sacred American rights. The right to petition.

Petition

The first P in RAPPS. The right to petition: "Congress shall make no law ... abridging ... the right of the people ... to petition the Government for a redress of grievances."

The right to petition is indeed the right to protest. In America, we are allowed to complain. Loudly. The First Amendment guarantees us the right to gather and protest against what we feel is unjust. The right to assembly allows us to do that in groups large enough to make a difference.

The rights of assembly and petition were tested again and again during the Civil Rights Movement protests of the 1950s and 1960s. In *Edwards v South Carolina* (1963), the Supreme Court overturned the breach of the peace conviction of 187 black high school and college students who had peacefully marched to protest segregation. In *Gregory v City of Chicago* (1969), the Court unanimously overturned the convictions of Comedian Dick Gregory and others who had participated in a march protesting the slow pace of desegregation in Chicago's public schools. Chief Justice Earl Warren, wrote that this was a "simple case." The protestors had been "charged and convicted for holding a demonstration." Their First Amendment rights to freedom of assembly and petition had been violated.

Anytime there is a protest, the protesters hope that there will be media coverage. This draws attention to their issue. And the great thing is, even if the government position or policy is not supportive of the protestors demands, the media can share their side of the story, because of the second P in RAPPS, freedom of the press.

Press

"Congress shall make no law ... abridging the freedom ... of the press."

One could argue that freedom of the press is our most important freedom. Traditionally, Americans have looked to the press to hold the government accountable. Without the news, how do we know what's happening? How do we decide who to vote for? How do we stay informed? Information comes from the press and if the government controls the press, the government controls the information. People in

North Korea are told by their government-controlled press that they live in a technologically advanced superpower that has repeatedly defeated the United States in battle, and is respected as a beacon of ethical behavior and intelligence around the world.

In 1971, the *New York Times* and the *Washington Post* began publishing a series of articles that quoted portions of a classified 7000-page report detailing U.S. military involvement in Vietnam from the end of the Second World War to May, 1968. The U.S. government tried to block the publication of these articles, arguing that they included top secret information, and their publication would endanger national security. In *New York Times Company v United States* (1971), in what became known as the Pentagon Papers Case, the Supreme Court ruled that the government did not have the right to block the publication of the papers. Justice Hugo Black, in concurring with the Court's decision, wrote:

> In the First Amendment, the Founding Fathers gave the free press the protection it must have to fulfill its essential role in our democracy. The press was to serve the governed, not the governors. The Government's power to censor the press was abolished so that the press would remain forever free to censure the Government. The press was protected so that it could bare the secrets of government and inform the people. Only a free and unrestrained press can effectively expose deception in government. And paramount among the responsibilities of a free press is the duty to prevent any part of the government from deceiving the people.

Of course, we no longer get our news by just reading the daily paper, or watching the six o'clock news on television. Today, in addition to newspapers and magazines, like *Newsweek* and *The Economist*, there is a never-ending stream of news coming from TV cable networks, like CNN and FOX, and from a seemingly limitless number of sources on the Internet. All this can make it very difficult to distinguish fact from opinion. Freedom of the press does not guarantee unbiased factual reporting of newsworthy events. Partisan news media, whether print, broadcast, or Internet, can present opinions as facts, choose to slant their coverage of a story, or even suppress it completely by not covering it.

Anyone with Internet access, or just a computer and a printer, can create their own version of the news, and promote the most absurd conspiracy theories. The Internet has opened a whole new can of proverbial worms. But censoring the press is a dangerous business especially because it starts us down a slippery slope to censoring free speech. Which brings us to the S in RAPPS, what most people think of first when they hear the First Amendment.

Speech

"Congress shall make no law ... abridging the freedom of speech." The fact is, this freedom is incredible. It allows us to speak our minds, and most importantly, to criticize and even make fun of our government's leaders. It underlies every other freedom we possess. In an address to the officers of his army, on March 15, 1783, George Washington said:

> For if men are to be precluded from offering their sentiments on a matter ... reason is of no use to us; the freedom of speech may be taken away, and, dumb and silent we may be led, like sheep, to the slaughter.

The freedom to speak freely is one that is not enjoyed by the citizens of every country. In China, Winnie the Pooh and depictions of the pants-less bear are banned. Some unsung genius noticed that Winnie the Pooh looks a lot like China's President Xi Jinping. So, in 2013, when Xi visited the United States, the person who first identified the resemblance between the loveable bear and Xi, posted an Internet meme showing Xi walking with President Obama and Pooh walking with Tigger. A few months later, when Xi met with Japanese Prime

Minister Shinzo Abe, a meme showing Xi shaking hands with Abe and Pooh shaking hands with Eeyore began circulating. Xi hit the roof. And the Chinese Communist Party, which doesn't seem to have a very good sense of humor, banned Winnie the Pooh. But more importantly, the Chinese people do not enjoy the right to free speech.

In China, and in many countries around the world, people end up in jail for expressing their opinion. Even when they are clearly making a joke. Every night on TV in the United States, we have comedians like Stephen Colbert and Trevor Noah making fun of our leaders. In other countries, they would be jailed for doing so. The Framers of the Constitution understood the importance of freedom of speech. They believed in the social contract theory, the idea that government serves the people. If the government is supposed to serve the people, then people have the right to criticize the government.

Americans have been criticizing their political leaders and those running for office since the very first days of the republic. A 1799 political cartoon depicted Thomas Jefferson kneeling at an altar and attempting to burn the Constitution. The cartoon conveyed the image that if Jefferson won the 1800 election, he would tear up the Constitution and rule as a dictator.

Freedom of speech means we have the freedom to disagree, to voice our own opinions, and most importantly to criticize and even make fun of our government. But that doesn't mean we are always going to like what others say, or that there are no limits to freedom of speech.

On June 9, 1990, in Fort Lauderdale, Florida, the police arrested a record shop owner, Charles Freeman, for selling a copy of 2 Live Crew's album, *As Nasty As They Wanna Be*. 2 Live Crew was a popular rap group in the 1990s. He was charged with distributing obscene material. The band's lead rapper Luther Cambell, aka Skyywalker, was known for profane lyrics, something Broward County Sheriff Nick Navarro didn't care for. He believed 2 Live Crew's music was profane and began arresting record store owners who sold the album.

Of course, there are lots of people who don't like profanity. Theodore Roosevelt, for example, thought that the English language was a magnificent medium through which to communicate and that only fools used profanity. But the issue wasn't whether you did or didn't like the use of profane language. The question was whether its use was protected by the First Amendment.

2 Live Crew lawyered up and filed suit in federal court, seeking a judicial declaration that their album was not obscene. Why? Because Sheriff Navarro was imposing an unconstitutional restraint on their right to free speech.

Federal District Court Judge Jose Gonzales described the case as a battle between two ancient enemies: "Anything Goes and Enough Already." He pointed out that Supreme Court Justice Oliver Wendell Holmes, Jr. had noted that the First Amendment's guarantee of freedom of speech is not absolute and that it does not, for example, permit someone to falsely yell "Fire" in a theater and cause a panic. Gonzales concluded that what he needed to decide was "whether the First Amendment absolutely permits one to yell the 'F' word anywhere in the community when combined with graphic sexual descriptions." In the end, he ruled that *As Nasty As They Wanna Be* was legally obscene, and therefore not entitled to First Amendment protections.

The judge arrived at his decision by applying what is known as the *Miller* test. In the United States, courts decide whether a work is obscene or not by answering the three questions posed by the Supreme Court in the 1973 *Miller v California* case.

How did we get that test? In 1971, Marvin Miller owned a store that sold adult films and books. Trying to drum up business, he got the bright idea to send out a brochure advertising his books and films. The brochure had graphic pictures. A woman who saw the brochure was so offended by the pictures that she called the police who promptly arrested Mr. Miller.

Miller was convicted of distributing obscene material. He appealed his conviction on the basis of his First Amendment rights, and the case eventually ended up in the lap of the highest court in the land. The question before the Supreme Court was whether the sale and distribution of obscene material was protected under the

First Amendment's guarantee of freedom of speech. And the verdict was no, it's not.

The Court ruled that "obscene material is not protected by the First Amendment". But now the problem was if obscene material isn't protected by the First Amendment, then what is obscene material? We need criteria. Enter the *Miller* test.

The Supreme Court's three necessary benchmarks which must be met for a work to be considered obscene and therefore subject to state regulation are: 1. Would the "the average person, applying contemporary community standards" find that the work, "taken as a whole," appeals to "prurient interest?" 2. Does the work depict or describe, in a patently offensive way, sexual conduct specifically defined by the applicable state law? 3. Does the work, "taken as a whole," lack serious literary, artistic, political, or scientific value?

That last one is where it gets tricky. Who gets to judge what does and doesn't have artistic value? There are people who don't like rap music. They think it's obscene. Florida District Court Judge Gonzales ruled that 2 Live Crew's album was obscene. But the 11th U.S. Circuit Court of Appeals found that the plaintiffs, 2 Live Crew, had submitted expert testimony that their album contained serious artistic value. The Court concluded: "A work cannot be held obscene unless each element of the *Miller* test has been met. We reject the argument that simply by listening to this musical work, the judge could determine that it had no serious artistic value."

But what about speech that incites violence? What about rap music that incites violence? In 1992, Texas Highway Patrol Trooper Bill Davidson stopped a man named Ronald Ray Howard for a broken tail light. As the trooper approached the car window, Howard opened fire with a 9-mm handgun, hitting Davidson in the neck and killing him.

Howard was listening to Tupac Shakur's *Soulja Story*. A rap song that talks about a man being pulled over by a cop, and then shooting him. In court, Howard claimed that the music had conditioned him to hate police officers and Tupac's lyrics motivated him to commit murder. The jury didn't buy Howard's explanation. He was convicted and sentenced to death. But this brought up an interesting question: Should lyrics that incite violence be protected as free speech?

Linda Davidson, the slain trooper's wife, didn't think so. She filed a civil suit against Tupac and his record label for millions of dollars in damages saying they were "grossly negligent in the distribution of *2pacalypse Now*." The album Howard was listening to when he murdered the trooper. Just like the murderer, Ronald Howard, Linda Davidson blamed the 2Pac's lyrics for her husband's death.

Then-Vice President Dan Quayle agreed. He called releasing the album "an irresponsible corporate act." But *2pacalypse Now* sold over a million copies. Clearly, it met the *Miller* test and a federal district court in Texas sided with Tupac Shakur against Linda Davidson, and ruled that the album was protected by the First Amendment. Regarding the incitement of violence, the court explained: "Calling one's music revolutionary does not, by itself, mean that Shakur intended his music to produce lawless conduct. At worst, Shakur's intent was to cause violence sometime after the listener considered Shakur's message. The First Amendment protects such advocacy."

In 1969, in *Brandenburg v Ohio*, the Supreme Court had sided with a Ku Klux Klan leader who had made a speech in which he called for industrial sabotage, violence, and other criminal acts. The Court ruled that "a state may not forbid speech advocating the use of force or unlawful conduct unless this advocacy is directed to inciting or producing imminent lawless action and is likely to incite or produce such action."

In reaching its decision, the Supreme Court recognized that prohibiting speech, even hateful and violent speech, is a slippery slope to censorship. After all, who is to say that video games and Hollywood movies don't incite violence. There have been cases made against all of them, from Ozzy Osbourne's lyrics promoting devil worship and drug use to the impact Grand Theft Auto and other video games may have on children. But in the end, the First Amendment protects it all under the freedom of speech umbrella.

What about libel? Does the First Amendment's guarantee of freedom of speech give you the right to say or publish things that are false and intended to damage a person's reputation? In 1960, the *New York Times* ran a full-page ad that criticized the Montgomery, Alabama police department. Some of the statements in the ad were not true. The police commissioner, L.B. Sullivan, sued the *Times,* claiming that he had been libeled by the false statements in the ad. The Alabama state courts sided with Sullivan, so the *Times* appealed to the Supreme Court. In *New York Times Company v Sullivan* (1964), the Court in a unanimous decision ruled in favor of the *Times.* As Justice William Brennan in the opinion for the Court explained:

> The constitutional guarantees require, we think, a federal rule that prohibits a public official from recovering damages for a defamatory falsehood relating to his official conduct unless he proves that the statement was made with "actual malice"—that is, with knowledge that it was false or with reckless disregard of whether it was false or not.

Social media has opened up a whole new can of worms when it comes to questions regarding the First Amendment's Free Speech guarantee. What about a high-school student who while off campus and after school hours posts vulgar images and messages with profane expletives on Facebook, Instagram, Snapchat, or some other social media platform. Are the student's posts protected speech, or does the school have a right to regulate student off-campus speech, and punish the student for the posts. In *Mahanoy Area School District v B.L.* (2021), the Supreme Court in an 8-1 decision affirmed a lower court ruling that Brandi Levy's (B.L.) First Amendment rights to freedom of speech had been violated when the School District punished her for social media posts that were made from an off-campus location after school hours. However, in the opinion for the Court, Justice

Stephen Breyer left the door open for school administrations to have some say in student off-campus speech:

> We do not now set forth a broad, highly general First Amendment rule stating just what counts as 'off campus' speech and whether or how ordinary First Amendment standards must give way off campus to a school's special need to prevent ... substantial disruption of learning-related activities or the protection of those who make up a school community.

Justice Samuel Alito, in a concurring opinion, described the "category of speech that is almost always beyond the regulatory authority of a public school."

> This is student speech that is not expressly and specifically directed at the school, school administrators, teachers, or fellow students and that addresses matters of public concern, including sensitive subjects like politics, religion, and social relations. Speech on such matters lies at the heart of the First Amendment's protection.

The First Amendment prevents the government from censoring speech, and that includes the presumption that the government will not pressure or coerce private parties to censor speech that disagrees with the government's policies. In a Special Message to Congress on August 8, 1950, President Truman wrote:

> Once a government is committed to the principle of silencing the voice of opposition, it has only one way to go, and that is down the path of increasingly repressive measures, until it becomes a source of terror to all its citizens and creates a country where everyone lives in fear.

On July 4, 2023, U.S. District Court Judge Terry A. Doughty issued a preliminary injunction barring the White House and several government agencies from having contact with social media companies for "the purpose of urging, encouraging, pressuring or inducing in any manner the removal, deletion, suppression or reduction of content containing protected free speech." In issuing his ruling, the Judge noted that beginning with the COVID-19 pandemic, "the United States Government seems to have assumed a role similar to an Orwellian 'Ministry of Truth.'" In George Orwell's novel, *1984*, the only viewpoints expressed by the media are the ones promulgated by the Ministry of Truth.

While the First Amendment prevents the government from censoring speech, it does not prohibit private entities from censoring speech. In 1996, Congress enacted Section 230 of the Communications Decency Act which provides social media platforms and other Internet service providers with protection from liability for "any action voluntarily taken in good faith to restrict access to or availability of material that the provider or user considers to be obscene, lewd, lascivious, filthy, excessively violent, harassing, or otherwise objectionable, whether or not such material is constitutionally protected."

On January 7, 2021, President Donald Trump's Facebook and Instagram accounts were suspended. The following day, the President was banned from Twitter. The reason that Meta, which owns Instagram and Facebook, and Twitter gave for their actions was that they believed that President Trump's posts and tweets, in the wake of what had happened at the Capitol on January 6, could, as the statement by Twitter explained, "be mobilized by different audiences, including to incite violence."

Two years later, on January 25, 2023, the Instagram and Facebook accounts of the former president, now a presidential candidate, were reinstated. His Twitter account had been reactivated in November 2022. Meta explained that it was ending Trump's suspension because "the public should be able to hear what their politicians are saying—the good, the bad and the ugly—so that they can make informed choices at the ballot box." The decisions both to ban the former President from social media platforms and then rescind the bans were very controversial.

Supreme Court Justice Louis D. Brandeis would have been opposed to allowing social media platforms to censor speech. In his classic concurring opinion in *Whitney v California* (1927), he wrote: "If there be time to expose through discussion, the falsehoods and fallacies, to avert the evil by the processes of education, the remedy to be applied is more speech, not enforced silence."

But what about outright lies? Xavier Alvarez made a regular habit of lying. He pretended to have played hockey for the Detroit Red Wings, retired from the Marine Corps after serving 25 years, been wounded multiple times in combat, and been awarded the Congressional Medal of Honor. That last lie was one too many, He was arrested, tried, and convicted of violating the Stolen Valor Act. He appealed his conviction, and in *United States v Alvarez* (2012), the Supreme Court ruled that the Stolen Valor Act, which made falsely claiming receipt of military ribbons or medals a criminal offense, violated the First Amendment's free speech protections.

Justice Anthony Kennedy in writing the opinion for the court cited Brandeis, and then added "The remedy for speech that is false is speech that is true. This is the ordinary course in a free society. The response to the unreasoned is the rational; to the uninformed, the enlightened; to the straight-out lie, the simple truth." He concluded his opinion by reminding us "that one of the costs of the First Amendment is that it protects the speech we detest as well as the speech we embrace."

Our First Amendment: The incredible freedoms of religion, assembly, petition, and speech that we are guaranteed and that most of us enjoy on a daily basis.

CHAPTER 2

BEARING ARMS: THE SECOND AMENDMENT

The Second Amendment guarantees the right to bear arms, that is the right to own firearms. It reads:

> A well regulated militia being necessary for the security of a free state, the right of the people to keep and bear arms shall not be infringed.

If you Google the Second Amendment and click on images, you will see pictures of guns and men holding guns with captions that read, "The Second Amendment is my gun permit. Don't tread on me"; "Protect the Second Amendment"; and "In guns we trust." While there also are pictures with captions that read, "Repeal the Second Amendment" and "Protect our Kids Not Guns," many of the pictures support the right of Americans to own firearms. Some people argue that gun ownership is as inherently American as turkey on Thanksgiving, and until relatively recently that was how the Second Amendment was interpreted. Of course, that interpretation is a little ambiguous, and that has been the source of recent controversy. Those who make the case that guns are engrained in U.S. culture aren't wrong. Indeed, you can make the case that it was the guns that the colonists owned that enabled Americans to win the war for independence.

But gun ownership, as we know, is a dual-edged sword. The United States has a higher rate of gun deaths than almost any other well to do nation. Statistics compiled by The University of Washington's

Institute for Health Metrics and Evaluation revealed that in 2021, the United States had 4.52 firearm homicides for every 100,000 people. That is over seven times the death rate from guns in Canada, nineteen times higher than in France, thirty-three times higher than in Australia, and seventy-seven times higher than in Germany. In 2021, eight percent of the deaths for those under 20 were attributable to gunshot wounds. The Center for Disease Control reported that 26,328 Americans used a gun to commit suicide in 2021. Another 20,958 were shot dead. Even more alarming is the fact that for each of the years 2020–2023, there have been over 600 mass shootings, which is an incident in which four or more people died of gunshot wounds. While every mass shooting is a tragedy, none are more horrifying than when school children and their teachers are the targets.

On May 24, 2022, an eighteen-year-old former student at the Robb Elementary School in Uvalde, Texas, went into the school and opened fire, killing nineteen children and two teachers, and wounding seventeen others. *Education Week* reported that there had been fifty-one school shootings in 2022, resulting in the deaths of thirty-two children and eight adults, and the wounding of 100 others. Clearly, gun violence is an issue in our country, and as a result, the debate about the Second Amendment has intensified.

When it comes to the debate about the Second Amendment, what it really comes down to is whether or not the Amendment protects the right of private individuals to keep and bear arms, or is it a right that can be exercised only through militia organizations like the National Guard. So, let's look at the language and think about the people who wrote it.

First things first—this Amendment appears to be all about a militia: "A well regulated militia, being necessary to the security of a free state, the right of the people to keep and bear arms shall not be infringed." In other words, because we need to make sure our militia is ready to rock and roll, people not only can have guns; they should have them. In 1791, this idea came straight from our recent experience fighting the British. But here's the thing about that. Yes, militias played a role in our victory but not a big one. In fact, if there's one lesson America learned from the rebellion against Britain, it's that a militia on its own was not enough to defend a country.

Without Washington's Continental Army, we would have lost the war, badly. But before you think, well OK great, let's have an army—armies have their own set of issues. The main one being that historically they had been used by governments to oppress people. Just look at what King George had done to the American colonists with his army. Armies can be used to keep governments in power, especially bad governments. Some of the Framers of the Constitution, particularly the Anti-Federalists, feared that. They feared that if our new government had an army, it might use that army to oppress the people.

To protect against this risk, the Anti-Federalists suggested that the government be permitted to raise armies of full-time paid troops only when needed to fight foreign adversaries. In other words, unless we were going to war, we wouldn't have an army. For other purposes, such as responding to emergencies, the government could rely on a militia that consisted of ordinary civilians who brought their own weapons and received some military training.

But at the Constitutional Convention, the Federalists had a more convincing argument: If we don't have an army, we are going to get slaughtered. The militias didn't win the Revolutionary War, the army did. And next time should we get invaded, or have to deal with some issues overseas, we better have professionals who are ready to handle that business. So, they decided that the federal government should have the authority to establish standing armies, even during peacetime, and to regulate the militia. Indeed, we still see that today, with our armed forces and what is our modern-day militia, the National Guard.

Naturally, Anti-Federalists were upset about this. They viewed it as a massive shift of power from the states to the federal government. They were scared that the proposed Constitution would take from the states their principal means of defense against the federal government should it become corrupt. The Federalists responded that fears of federal oppression were overblown because the American people were armed, and they would be almost impossible to subdue through military force. But the question is, was that true? Would an armed citizenry be able to stop an oppressive government should the need arise?

And that's really what the Federalists and Anti-Federalists were disagreeing over: whether or not an armed populace could adequately deter federal oppression. Because implicit in the debate they were having were two shared assumptions. First, the proposed new Constitution gave the federal government almost total legal authority over the army and militia. Second, the federal government should not have any authority at all to disarm the citizenry. The Amendment was accepted because of almost unanimous agreement that the federal government should not have the power to infringe the right of the people to keep and bear arms. It could also be viewed as a concession to the states that in that it allowed them to form militias. Today, every state has a National Guard—a state-based military force that derives its authority from the Second Amendment.

Of course, much has changed since 1791. The traditional militia fell into desuetude, and state-based militia organizations like the National Guard were eventually incorporated into the federal military structure. America's military establishment has become much more powerful than any eighteenth-century person could have possibly imagined. In this day and age, does anyone really believe that an armed citizenry can stand up to the U.S. armed forces in battle? Even if we respect a militia member who belongs to what University of Hartford professor Robert Churchill calls a "constitutionalist" group—men who believe it is their patriotic duty to stand up for the limited government the Framers of the Constitution envisaged, and oppose the ever-expanding powers of the federal government—if his group went up against a U.S. Army Ranger squad, the smart money would be on the Rangers.

So why did the Anti-Federalists agree to a standing army? Probably because they couldn't envision the future. In the eighteenth-century civilians routinely kept at home the very same weapons they would use if called to serve in the militia. They had muskets for protection from bears and bobcats and to shoot rabbits and other cute woodland critters for stew. But that's all changed. Americans don't need to shoot anything to eat for dinner. And, given the amazing weapons modern soldiers are equipped with, civilians are no longer expected to use their household weapons for militia duty.

But now the question has become, even if they aren't expected to furnish their own weapons for militia duty, do they have the right to own and keep such weapons? And here's where the argument gets tricky. There is nothing in the Second Amendment about the specific types of firearms U.S. citizens can keep or be prohibited from bearing. In the 1700s, the citizens had the same weapons as the military. The farmer and the soldier used the same musket. Today, that's different. I doubt the Framers of the Constitution could have predicted future mass shootings when the hottest weapon of the day was a flintlock musket that took thirty seconds to be reloaded after every shot.

And yet, if the whole point of the Second Amendment was for citizens to be armed well enough to protect themselves from the potential tyranny of a corrupt government and its army, then if that is what the Framers were really thinking, should someone be able to have Tomahawk missiles mounted on his back porch? First, it would be awesome for intimidating neighbors, and it would be more in line with what the Anti-Federalists wanted. If our government got out of hand, those missiles would go a lot further in helping to defend against the U.S. military than the Remington rifle sold at Walmart.

No one is seriously suggesting that civilians should have access to whatever weaponry the government has, the way your average citizen did in the 1700s when the Second Amendment was written. The Framers—Anti Federalists and Federalists—agreed the citizenry must have the right to bear arms to protect against a government, with an army, that becomes oppressive. Especially our own. But now, our government has such a powerful military and such advanced weaponry that even a well-armed citizenry could never possibly stand up to it.

Of course, guns are still prevalent in America because the Second Amendment guarantees the right to keep and bear arms. According to the Geneva-based Small Arms Survey, in 2018, there were 393 million privately owned firearms in the United States. Needless to say, which guns you can own and for what purpose you can have them is the subject of heated interpretation and heated debate.

Exercising its power to levy taxes, Congress in 1934 enacted the National Firearms Act, which imposed a tax on the making and transfer of machine guns, silencers, and rifles and shotguns with barrels that were less than eighteen inches in length. The act also included requirements for the registration of certain firearms. The registration provisions of the National Firearms Act were invalidated by the Supreme Court in the 1968 case, *Haynes v United States*.

In *United States v Miller* (1939), the Supreme Court unanimously held that Congress could prohibit the possession of a sawed-off shotgun because that sort of weapon had no "reasonable relationship to the preservation or efficiency of a 'well regulated militia.'" It is interesting that the Court used the militia argument as a way to restrict the use of a weapon which most reasonable people would agree is mostly purposed for assassinations. *Miller* set the precedent that the only weapons that could not be regulated by the government were those whose "use could contribute to the common defense" as part of the kit of a well-regulated militia.

Following the assassinations of Robert Kennedy and Dr. Martin Luther King, Jr. Congress passed the Gun Control Act in 1968. The act banned mail order sales of firearms, and made it a federal offense to sell a gun to a felon, drug user, or a mentally disabled person. It also required that manufacturers and dealers involved in the interstate shipment or sales of firearms obtain a Federal Firearms License. The Brady Handgun Prevention Act added the requirements of a five-day waiting period and a background check before a federally licensed firearms dealer could sell a firearm.

In two recent landmark cases, the Supreme Court has clawed back regulations on private gun ownership. In *District of Columbia v Heller* (2008), the Court ruled that a DC law was unconstitutional because the law violated the provisions of the Second Amendment. The law virtually banned all private ownership of firearms, and also required that guns kept at home would have to be rendered non-functional. Writing for the majority, Justice Antonin Scalia expressed the view that the Second Amendment guarantees the "right to possess and carry weapons" for protection. He wrote: "The inherent right of self-defense has been central to the Second Amendment right."

Gun control advocates point to the fact that Scalia also wrote that the Second Amendment does not convey the "right to keep and carry any weapon whatsoever in any manner whatsoever and for whatever purpose." He noted that "nothing in our opinion should be taken to cast doubt on longstanding prohibitions on the possession of firearms by felons and the mentally ill, or laws forbidding the carrying of firearms in sensitive places such as schools and government buildings, or laws imposing conditions and qualifications on the commercial sale of arms."

In 2022, in *New York State Rifle and Pistol Association v Bruen*, the Supreme Court invalidated a New York law that required a person applying for a concealed permit license to prove that he or she had a valid need for self-defense protections not enjoyed by the general public. In the majority opinion, Justice Clarence Thomas stated that the Second Amendment protects

> an individual's right to carry a handgun for self-defense outside the home." He held "that when the Second Amendment's plain text covers an individual's conduct, the Constitution presumptively protects that conduct. To justify its regulation, the government may not simply posit that the regulation promotes an important interest. Rather, the government must demonstrate that the regulation is consistent with this Nation's historical tradition of firearm regulation ... The government must affirmatively prove that its firearms regulation is part of the historical tradition that delimits the outer bounds of the right to keep and bear arms.

Thomas concluded by noting that if the Court were to uphold the New York law, it would be treating the Second Amendment differently than it treats other constitutional rights. Referring to the First Amendment's freedom of speech guarantee, he wrote that when the "Government restricts speech, the Government bears the burden of proving the constitutionality of its actions."

If *Bruen* gives each of us the presumptive right to wear a Glock in our shoulder holster, the opinion of the Fifth Circuit Court of Appeals in *United States v Daniels* (2023) gives drug users and alcoholics the right to purchase a gun as long as they are not smoking weed, sniffing cocaine, or stumbling down drunk at the time of the sale. Patrick Daniels had been convicted of violating the federal law that bars an "unlawful user" of a controlled substance from owning a firearm. Daniels was a regular user of marijuana, but the government had presented no evidence that he was using weed when he purchased his gun. Daniels appealed, and the Fifth Circuit overturned his conviction. The Court, relying on *Bruen*, concluded that the law violated Daniels' Second Amendment rights because it was inconsistent with the nation's "historical tradition of firearm regulation."

While the majority opinion in *Bruen* acknowledged that throughout "American history, laws have regulated the combination of guns and intoxicating substances." The three-judge panel concluded that the government had at no time in America's history disarmed

> individuals who used drugs or alcohol at one time from possessing guns at another... the first federal law of its kind— was not enacted until 1968, nearly two centuries after the Second Amendment was adopted. In short, our history and tradition may support some limits on an intoxicated person's right to carry a weapon, but it does not justify disarming a sober citizen based exclusively on his past drug usage. Nor do more generalized traditions of disarming dangerous persons support this restriction on nonviolent drug users.

In September 2023, Hunter Biden, President Biden's son, was indicted on three felony counts related to his purchase of a firearm in October 2018, while he was a drug user. His lawyers, relying on *Bruen* and *Daniels* argued that the statute federal prosecutors used to charge Hunter is unconstitutional. The Supreme Court will have to eventually decide whether prohibitions on the purchase of firearms generally apply to drug users, or only apply when the user is under the influence.

The Supreme Court in *United States v Rahimi* (2024) in an 8–1 decision ruled that the Violence Against Women Act provision that prohibits someone who is under a domestic violence restraining order from owning a gun did not violate the Second Amendment's right to bear arms. As Chief Justice John Roberts, in the opinion for the Court, explained, "Our tradition of firearm regulation allows the Government to disarm individuals who present a credible threat to the physical safety of others."

In the recent wake of several mass shootings and increased gun violence in major U.S. cities, the debate over gun ownership has become very heated. The gulf between the National Rifle Association that rejects any laws regulating gun ownership and organizations like the Brady Campaign and the Giffords Center to Prevent Gun Violence could not be wider.

The Second Amendment: A well regulated militia being necessary for the security of a free state, the right of the people to keep and bear arms shall not be infringed.

Reflective of the time in which it was written and a catalyst for debate and controversy. Then and now.

CHAPTER 3

INNOCENT UNTIL PROVEN GUILTY: THE THIRD THROUGH EIGHTH AMENDMENTS

The Third, Fourth, Fifth, Sixth, Seventh, and Eighth Amendments guarantee that Americans enjoy protections against unreasonable searches and seizures, have the right to a jury trial, and cannot be subjected to cruel and unusual punishments.

The Third Amendment: Your Home is Not a Barracks

The Third Amendment reads:

No soldier shall, in time of peace be quartered in any house, without the consent of the owner, nor in time of war, but in a manner to be prescribed by law.

This means that we cannot be forced to house or quarter soldiers. So why do we have the Third Amendment? Because of the British. Between 1754 and 1763, the British Empire sent thousands of soldiers to its American colonies to fight in the French and Indian War. After the war, many of these soldiers continued to be stationed in America because Britain felt it needed to maintain a standing army in its North American colonies. In 1765, the British Parliament passed the Quartering Act requiring the colonists to provide food and housing to soldiers stationed in their towns and villages. Needless to say, this act was unpopular in the colonies, especially after the 1770 Boston Massacre in which British troops fired on a crowd and killed five colonists.

In 1774, the British Parliament, in the wake of the Boston Tea Party, enacted another Quartering Act as a coercive measure. This one required colonists to allow British soldiers to take up residence in their private homes. The forced quartering of soldiers was among the grievances Thomas Jefferson listed in the Declaration of Independence. Specifically, he accused King George III of keeping "among us, in Times of Peace, Standing Armies, without the Consent or of our Legislatures," and "quartering large Bodies of Armed Troops among us."

So, we all know the history. The colonists win their independence. The British are expelled, and in 1787, the constitutional Framers get to work on writing the supreme law of the land. They debated whether the United States should even have a standing army. We know that from our discussion of the Second Amendment. We also know the Federalists won that debate. Ultimately, the Framers decided that a standing army was a necessary evil—how else could we protect our new nation? But the Framers were so concerned with how the British army had recently treated their American subjects that they wanted it to be clear that the role of our soldiers would be only to repel foreign threats, not to enforce laws against U.S. citizens.

James Madison wrote the Third Amendment of the Bill of Rights in order to guarantee that the federal government couldn't force local governments, businesses, and citizens to house U.S. soldiers. In the years following the ratification of the Constitution, military troops were sometimes used to fight forest fires and provide humanitarian assistance in the wake of natural disasters such as floods, tornadoes, and hurricanes. But they were rarely used for routine law enforcement. A notable exception was what has become known as the Little Rock Crisis.

In September 1957, nine black school children tried to enroll in Little Rock's Central High School. The governor of Arkansas, Orval Faubus, ordered the Arkansas National Guard to surround the school and prevent the children from entering it. President Eisenhower, issued an executive order placing the Guard under federal control, and ordered troops of the 101st Airborne Division to Little Rock to protect the children and ensure that they could enroll in the school and safely attend classes there.

More recently, in March 2021, Governor Greg Abbott of Texas launched Operation Lone Star and began deploying Texas National Guard troops to secure portions of the border between the United States and Mexico.

Still, it's not like soldiers are going to be showing up at your door wanting dinner and asking to crash on your couch. Since the Third Amendment's ratification in 1791, the U.S. Supreme Court has only mentioned it a couple of times.

The Third Amendment was cited in the 1965 landmark Supreme Court case, *Griswold v Connecticut*. In this case, the Court ruled that an 1879 Connecticut law banning the use of contraceptive drugs or devices was unconstitutional because it violated the right of individuals to privacy. Justice William O. Douglas, in the majority opinion, argued that the First, Third, Fourth, and Ninth Amendments all implied a constitutionally protected right to privacy. Referring to the Third Amendment, he wrote, "its prohibition against the quartering of soldiers 'in any house' in time of peace without the consent of the owner is another facet of that privacy."

The most famous case involving the Third Amendment is often referred to as the Steel Seizure Case. In 1952, at the height of the Korean War, with U.S. supplies of military equipment running low, the United Steel Workers of America were planning to strike. President Truman argued that producing the steel needed for guns, tanks, and planes was more important than allowing steel workers to try to gain a more favorable contract by striking. He issued an executive order that directed the Secretary of Commerce, Charles Sawyer, to seize and operate most of the country's steel mills.

Truman's order to seize and operate steel mills didn't sit well with the Youngstown Sheet and Tube Company. They complied with the president's order but also started a legal battle that eventually ended up on the Supreme Court's docket as *Youngstown Sheet & Tube Company v Sawyer*. The Court ruled that the president didn't have the authority to seize private property without an act of Congress. In writing the opinion for the majority, Justice Robert Jackson cited the Third Amendment as justification for overruling Truman's order. He wrote, "Even in war time, his seizure of needed military housing must be authorized by Congress."

So, does that mean that Congress can order Americans to quarter soldiers during times of war? The answer is yes. Congress can order Americans to house troops during times of war. It's not likely to ever happen but the last line of the Amendment, "in a manner to be prescribed by law" indicates it could. For example, Congress, in an emergency, could pass a law requiring private citizens to quarter troops because we are facing a national crisis.

But, it's pretty unlikely. Indeed, the Third Amendment is one of the least controversial, least debated, and least cited sections of the Constitution. In the words of Encyclopedia Britannica "as the history of the country progressed with little conflict on American soil, the Amendment has had little occasion to be invoked." And while the Amendment has been used to justify a few Supreme Court decisions like *Youngstown v Sawyer* and *Griswold v Connecticut*, the Amendment itself has never been the primary basis of a ruling.

In *Engblom v Carey* (1982), the United States Court of Appeals for the Second Circuit ruled that National Guard troops fall under the Third Amendment's definition of soldiers. Citing that ruling in 2015, the U.S. District Court for the District of Nevada, in the case of *Mitchell v City of Henderson, Nevada*, ruled that Mitchells' Third Amendment rights were not violated when the police occupied their home because police officers are not soldiers. Which raises an interesting question. If the right to bear arms guaranteed by the Second Amendment is an inherent right, not one tied to a militia-related requirement, then why isn't the Third Amendment's right to protection against quartering also an inherent right, one that should provide protection against home invasions by anyone, not just by soldiers?

The Third Amendment, infrequently cited, but not irrelevant.

The Fourth Amendment:
Your Home is Your Castle

The Constitution, through the Fourth Amendment, protects people from unreasonable searches and seizures by the government. It reads:

> The right of the people to be secure in their persons, houses, papers, and effects, against unreasonable searches and seizures, shall not be violated, and no Warrants shall issue, but upon probable cause, supported by Oath or affirmation, and particularly describing the place to be searched, and the persons or things to be seized.

Introduced in 1789, the Fourth Amendment struck at the heart of a matter central to the early American experience: the principle that, within reason, "Every man's house is his castle." In 1763, the issue had come to a head in the British House of Commons when members rose to speak in opposition to a law the British government had enacted that allowed sheriffs and tax collectors to search homes and other private property without a warrant. William Pitt expressed the view that a man's home is his castle in these words:

> The poorest man may, in his cottage, bid defiance to all the forces of the Crown. It may be frail; its roof may shake; the wind may blow through it; the storm may enter, the rain may enter, but the King of England may not enter.

According to the National Bureau of Economic Research's working paper on urbanization in the United States, prior to 1830, only about 10% of the U.S. population lived in towns and cities. In the late eighteenth and early nineteenth centuries, most Americans lived on farms in homes which they had very likely built with wood from trees they had felled in the process of clearing the land they now farmed. So it's no surprise that they viewed their homes as their castles.

The Founders understood that any citizen could fall into the category of the criminally accused and ought to be provided protections accordingly. Especially because the British had used writs of assistance to search the homes and other property of the colonists, and even the colonists themselves. These writs gave the British authorities the ability to search whoever and whatever they wished, with or without probable cause.

The Fourth Amendment, however, is not a guarantee against all searches and seizures, but only those that are unreasonable and executed without probable cause. In other words, the Fourth Amendment protects us from illegal searches and seizures conducted by police and other government officials. While the Third Amendment has rarely been cited in court cases, the Fourth Amendment has been at the forefront of over one hundred cases heard by the Supreme Court, and at issue in a great many more cases heard by the lower courts.

In *Weeks v United States* (1914), Justice William Day delivered the unanimous verdict of the Supreme Court that the Fourth Amendment rights of Fremont Weeks had been violated. He began his opinion by summarizing the facts of the case:

> The defendant was arrested by a police officer, so far as the record shows, without warrant, at the Union Station in Kansas City, Missouri, where he was employed by an express company. Other police officers had gone to the house of the defendant, and being told by a neighbor where the key was kept, found it and entered the house. They searched the defendant's room and took possession of various papers and articles found there, which were afterwards turned over to the United States marshal. Later in the same day, police officers returned with the marshal, who thought he might find additional evidence and, being admitted by someone in the house...the marshal searched the defendant's room... Neither the marshal nor the police officer had a search warrant.

The letters and envelopes that the police officers and the U.S. marshal found in the Weeks's room were used to convict Weeks of violating the Kansas City Criminal Code by transporting lottery tickets through the mail. Weeks wanted his papers back, and the Supreme Court agreed that he should get them back and that they should not have been used as evidence at Week's trial. As Justice Day explained:

> The effect of the Fourth Amendment is to put the courts of the United States and Federal officials, in the exercise of their power and authority, under limitations and restraints as to the exercise of such power and authority, and to forever secure the people, their persons, houses, papers, and effects, against all unreasonable searches and seizures under the guise of law. This protection reaches all alike, whether accused of crime or not, and the duty of giving to it force and effect is obligatory upon all entrusted under our Federal system with the enforcement of the laws. The tendency of those who execute the criminal laws of the country to obtain conviction by means of unlawful seizures and enforced confessions, the latter often obtained after subjecting accused persons to unwarranted practices destructive of rights secured by the Federal Constitution, should find no sanction in the judgments of the courts, which are charged at all times with the support of the Constitution, and to which people of all conditions have a right to appeal for the maintenance of such fundamental rights.

Weeks gave rise to what is known as the Exclusionary Rule: Evidence obtained through an illegal search or seizure is inadmissible at trial. Even if the evidence makes a prima facie case for a person's guilt, it cannot be used at trial. What if the police recover the knife a husband used to slit the throat of his wife? The knife has her blood and his fingerprints on it. The evidence is conclusive that this is the murder weapon, and he is the murderer. But if the knife was recovered as the result of an illegal search, then it cannot be presented as evidence at his trial, and if there is no other compelling evidence, he gets away with murder.

In 1939, Supreme Court Justice Felix Frankfurter, in *Nardone v United States*, described evidence that was obtained legally, but might not have otherwise been discovered but for a prior illegal search as "the fruit of the poisonous tree." If during an illegal search, the police find the key to a safe deposit box, and then obtain a warrant to search the contents of that box, the evidence collected from the box would be considered the fruit of a poisonous tree, and in accordance with the Exclusionary Rule could not be used by the prosecution at trial. However, if the prosecution can prove that the evidence obtained through an illegal search would have eventually been obtained through legal means, the evidence may be admissible. But proving that the illegally seized evidence would inevitably have been discovered legally is a pretty high bar to jump.

There are three generally accepted exceptions to the Exclusionary Rule as it applies to the Fourth Amendment:

1. A warrant is not required if someone agrees to be searched or allows you to search his home, car, or other property.
2. Police may search someone they are arresting and that person's immediate surroundings.
3. The evidence seized by the police was in plain view, e.g., the officer sees 50 kilos of meth in the cargo area of an SUV he has stopped for speeding.

The Exclusionary Rule was initially applied only in federal courts. State courts relied on a common law convention that all evidence was admissible no matter how obtained. But in *Mapp v Ohio* (1961), the Supreme Court ruled that the Exclusionary Rule applied not just to federal prosecutions but to state ones as well. Thus, the obscene materials the police found in Dollree Mapp's home as the result of an illegal search should not have been admitted into evidence, and her conviction had to be overturned. As Justice Thomas Clark, in the majority opinion explained:

> Presently, a federal prosecutor may make no use of evidence illegally seized, but a State's attorney across the street may,

although he supposedly is operating under the enforceable prohibitions of the same Amendment. Thus, the State, by admitting evidence unlawfully seized, serves to encourage disobedience to the Federal Constitution which it is bound to uphold.

Charles Katz used a public phone booth to inform bookies of his handicaps. He was arrested for violating a federal law that made it illegal to transmit betting information across state lines. The evidence used to obtain a conviction were recordings of his telephone conversations. Federal agents had wiretapped the phone in the booth that he used. Katz appealed his conviction and the Supreme Court agreed that his Fourth Amendment rights had been violated. Writing the opinion for the Court, Justice Potter Stewart concluded that by listening to and recording Katz's words without first having secured a warrant permitting them to do so, the agents "violated the privacy on which he justifiably relied while using the telephone booth and thus constituted a 'search and seizure' within the meaning of the Fourth Amendment." In other words, the Fourth Amendment applied not just to the search and seizure of physical objects, it also included a right to privacy.

In a concurring opinion, Justice John Harlan, concluded that the protections afforded by the Fourth Amendment were subject to a twofold requirement:

> First that a person have exhibited an actual (subjective) expectation of privacy and, second, that the expectation be one that society is prepared to recognize as "reasonable". Thus a man's home is, for most purposes, a place where he expects privacy, but objects, activities, or statements that he exposes to the "plain view" of outsiders are not "protected" because no intention to keep them to himself has been exhibited. On the other hand, conversations in the open would not be protected against being overheard, for the expectation of privacy under the circumstances would be unreasonable.

Private speech is protected, but what if the police obtain a record of what you said, texted or emailed to another person, and then try to use that to incriminate you? Is your speech still protected if it is obtained from a third party?

On October 4, 2009, Trisha Oliver called 911 from her Cranston, Rhode Island apartment when her six-year-old son Marco Nieves stopped breathing. The EMTs arrived a few minutes later, and took the boy in an ambulance to Hasbro Children's Hospital, where he died eleven hours later.

Sergeant Michael Kite of the Cranston Police Department arrived at the apartment shortly after the ambulance had left for the hospital. He met with the child's mother, Trisha Oliver, and her boyfriend Michael Patino. Kite noticed a cell phone on the kitchen counter, picked it up and read the text messages that were on it.

The phone was owned by the child's mother, Trisha Oliver. She had sent a message to her boyfriend Michael Patino which read, "Wat if I got 2 take him 2 da hospital wat do I say and dos marks on his neck omg." It wasn't just the English language that was being murdered that night; Oliver had watched her boyfriend beat her son to death. There were other messages on Trisha's phone, and some of them referred to beatings Marco had received. Based on the text messages and other evidence the police collected, including cell phone and landline records, and Patino's confession that he had beaten Marco, Trisha's boyfriend Michael Patino was arrested and charged with the murder of Trisha's six-year-old son.

Virtually all of the evidence the police obtained was deemed inadmissible because of the Exclusionary Rule. Rhode Island Superior Court Associate Justice Judith Savage ruled that it was "tainted by the illegal search made by Sgt. Kite or the other illegal searches and seizures of cell phones and their contents." Which begs the question: What if we have to let the Michael Patino's of the world go free? Even when we know they are guilty? How much do we value the Fourth Amendment and our right to be secure in our homes and effects against unreasonable searches and seizures? So much so that we let murderers walk?

The state appealed the decision to throw out the evidence against Patino. The Rhode Island Supreme Court (2014) began its analysis of the case by noting that "the central question confronting us ... is relatively narrow, whether a person has a reasonable expectation of privacy in his or her text messages stored in a cell phone belonging to, or possessed by, another person." The Court reversed Justice Savage's ruling on the grounds that Fourth Amendment protections do not extend to information given to a third party.

> In determining whether a person has an expectation of privacy in his text messages, the most important factor, in our opinion, is from whose phone the messages are accessed. Underlying this consideration is the element of control; that is to say, when the recipient receives the message, the sender relinquishes control over what becomes of that message on the recipient's phone.

Michael Patino was re-tried, convicted of murder, and sentenced to life imprisonment. Sometimes, justice is served.

The Rhode Island Supreme Court's decision was in keeping with what is known as the third-party doctrine, which holds that a person has no expectation of privacy in information voluntarily shared with others, or in records maintained by others. In the 1976 case, *Miller v United States*, the Supreme Court had decided that bank records were owned by the bank and that an individual depositor did not enjoy Fourth Amendment protections with respect to records of his financial transactions. In *Smith v Maryland* (1979), it ruled that since an individual must inform his phone company of the numbers that he is calling in order for the calls to be connected, he therefore has no reason to expect that those numbers will be kept private.

In other words, if you sent the message, it's now on someone else's phone and you can't expect that person to keep it private for you. Indeed, the Fourth Amendment was written before the digital age. Cell phones and emails have added a whole new set of challenges to our Fourth Amendment rights. Both Justices Potter Stewart and

Thurgood Marshall understood this as they explained in their dissenting opinions in *Smith*. Justice Stewart wrote:

> The numbers dialed from a private telephone—although certainly more prosaic than the conversation itself—are not without "content." Most private telephone subscribers may have their own numbers listed in a publicly distributed directory, but I doubt there are any who would be happy to have broadcast to the world a list of the local or long distance numbers they have called. This is not because such a list might in some sense be incriminating, but because it easily could reveal the identities of the persons and the places called, and thus reveal the most intimate details of a person's life.

Justice Marshall expressed an even greater concern:

> Privacy in placing calls is of value not only to those engaged in criminal activity. The prospect of unregulated governmental monitoring will undoubtedly prove disturbing even to those with nothing illicit to hide. Many individuals, including members of unpopular political organizations or journalists with confidential sources, may legitimately wish to avoid disclosure of their personal contacts.... Permitting governmental access to telephone records on less than probable cause may thus impede certain forms of political affiliation and journalistic endeavor that are the hallmark of a truly free society.

The third-party doctrine is not cast in stone. *Carpenter v United States* (2018) was a case that involved the cell-site location information (CSLI) of Timothy Carpenter's phone. Federal agents had used that information, which they had obtained without a warrant from Carpenter's cell phone service provider, to track his movements over a 127-day period. In all, they had used 12,898 location points, an average of 101 data points a day, to place him near the scene of four robberies at the time the robberies occurred. The Court, in this case, decided that a warrant was required and the evidence collected by the agents was inadmissible. However, Chief Justice Roberts left the third-party doctrine door open:

> Not all orders compelling the production of documents will require a showing of probable cause. A warrant is required only in the rare case where the suspect has a legitimate privacy interest in records held by a third party. And even though the Government will generally need a warrant to access CSLI, case-specific exceptions—e.g., exigent circumstances—may support a warrantless search.

One of the challenges the courts are having to deal with is whether in the interest of national security, our Fourth Amendment rights are being violated without our knowledge. The men and women who work at the National Security Agency at Fort Meade, Maryland, or at CIA headquarters in McLean, Virginia, are required to check their cell phones at the door. Because cell phones can be monitored. Never have any doubt that a cell phone, even if it's off, can be turned on remotely and used to listen, see, and record your conversations by the intelligence agencies of almost every developed country in the world. This is something that all new State Department hires are told on their first day on the job.

Phone data—where you have been, who you have called, who you have received calls and texts from—is even easier to access. Which is all well and good that the U.S. Government can spy on other nations, but what about when they are spying on us?

On October 26, 2001, Congress passed a bill, signed into law by President George W. Bush, known as the Patriot Act. It was a reaction to the terrorist attacks on September 11, 2001. The Act was designed to enhance law enforcement investigatory tools and protect America from future attacks. Title 2 of the Act opened a can of constitutional worms. Under "Enhanced Surveillance Procedures," it authorized government agencies to gather foreign intelligence from both U.S. and non-U.S. citizens. The Patriot Act included provisions allowing expanded wiretapping, the interception and use of private communications, and the release of electronic communications, such as cell phone metadata, to law enforcement and intelligence agencies.

On September 18, 2014, President Obama's Director of National Intelligence, James Clapper, had this to say about the data being collected by the intelligence agencies:

> We are expected to keep the nation safe and provide exquisite, high-fidelity, timely, accurate, anticipatory, and relevant intelligence; and do that in such a manner that there is no risk; and there is no embarrassment to anyone if what we're doing is publicly revealed; and there is no threat to anyone's revenue bottom line; and there isn't even a scintilla of jeopardy to anyone's civil liberties and privacy, whether U.S. persons or foreign persons. We call this new approach to intelligence: "immaculate collection."

The American Civil Liberties Union didn't think "immaculate collection" was funny. It filed suit. The ACLU argued that a secret order from the Foreign Intelligence Surveillance Court requiring Verizon "to turn over on "an ongoing daily basis" phone call details including whom calls are placed to and from, when those calls are made, and how long they last" was a violation of the Fourth Amendment because such "information, known as metadata, can reveal intimate details about our private lives." Congress agreed, and in 2015, passed the Freedom Act, which ended the bulk collection of metadata.

In response to what he believed was having his hands tied behind his back, and preventing him from doing the job he thought would keep America safe, Clapper said this:

> The result of this perfect storm is that we, as a nation, are taking more risk. In many cases, we've chosen where we're taking risk—cutting specific programs, stopping specific collections,

declassifying specific documents. All of those are good choices, as long as we recognize that we, as a nation, have to manage the attendant risks that we will incur when we take these actions.

Which begs the crucial question surrounding the Fourth Amendment, which do we as a people value more, our privacy or our security? Benjamin Franklin famously said, "Those who would give up essential liberty to purchase a little temporary safety deserve neither liberty nor safety." More recently (2013), President Obama said, "I think it's important to understand that you can't have 100 percent security and then have 100 percent privacy and zero inconvenience." But perhaps Justice Sonia Sotomayor best expressed the concerns that many Americans have when in her dissent to *United States v Jones* (2012), a case involving the use of a GPS tracker that had been secretly installed on the defendant's car, she wrote:

> I would ask whether people reasonably expect that their movements will be recorded and aggregated in a manner that enables the Government to ascertain, more or less at will, their political and religious beliefs, sexual habits, and so on.... More fundamentally, it may be necessary to reconsider the premise that an individual has no reasonable expectation of privacy in information voluntarily disclosed to third parties.... People disclose the phone numbers that they dial or text to their cellular providers; the URLs that they visit and the e-mail addresses with which they correspond to their Internet service providers; and the books, groceries, and medications they purchase to online retailers....I for one doubt that people would accept without complaint the warrantless disclosure to the Government of a list of every Web site they had visited in the last week, or month, or year. But whatever the societal expectations, they can attain constitutionally protected status only if our Fourth Amendment jurisprudence ceases to treat secrecy as a prerequisite for privacy. I would not assume that all information voluntarily disclosed to some member of the

public for a limited purpose is, for that reason alone, disentitled to Fourth Amendment protection.

In concluding the majority opinion for the Court in *Terry v Ohio* (1968), which involved the question of whether police have the right to stop and frisk citizens that they suspect might be armed or likely to engage in illegal activities, Chief Justice Earl Warren wrote:

> Where a police officer observes unusual conduct which leads him reasonably to conclude in light of his experience that criminal activity may be afoot and that the persons with whom he is dealing may be armed and presently dangerous, where, in the course of investigating this behavior, he identifies himself as a policeman and makes reasonable inquiries, and where nothing in the initial stages of the encounter serves to dispel his reasonable fear for his own or others' safety, he is entitled for the protection of himself and others in the area to conduct a carefully limited search of the outer clothing of such persons in an attempt to discover weapons which might be used to assault him.
>
> Such a search is a reasonable search under the Fourth Amendment, and any weapons seized may properly be introduced in evidence against the person from whom they were taken.

Justice William O. Douglas concluded his dissenting opinion in *Terry* with the following admonition:

> The infringement on personal liberty of any "seizure" of a person can only be "reasonable" under the Fourth Amendment if we require the police to possess "probable cause" before they seize him. Only that line draws a meaningful distinction between an officer's mere inkling and the presence of facts within the officer's personal knowledge which would convince a reasonable man that the person seized has committed, is committing, or is about to commit a particular crime.

There have been powerful hydraulic pressures throughout our history that bear heavily on the Court to water down constitutional guarantees and give the police the upper hand. That hydraulic pressure has probably never been greater than it is today.

Yet if the individual is no longer to be sovereign, if the police can pick him up whenever they do not like the cut of his jib, if they can "seize" and "search" him in their discretion, we enter a new regime. The decision to enter it should be made only after a full debate by the people of this country.

The debate over the Fourth Amendment is still on-going.

The Fifth Amendment:
You Have the Right to Remain Silent

Everyone has heard someone say, "I plead the Fifth." It's in almost every courtroom drama and police show on television. It is a part of our culture, simultaneously perhaps our most known and yet least understood right. It reads:

> No person shall be held to answer for a capital, or otherwise infamous crime, unless on a presentment or indictment of a Grand Jury, except in cases arising in the land or naval forces, or in the Militia, when in actual service in time of War or public danger; nor shall any person be subject for the same offence to be twice put in jeopardy of life or limb; nor shall be compelled in any criminal case to be a witness against himself, nor be deprived of life, liberty, or property, without due process of law; nor shall private property be taken for public use, without just compensation.

First and foremost, if you're being held in jail for an infamous crime, a major crime, a Grand Jury, made up of a group of ordinary citizens, needs to suspect that you are guilty and wants you tried. If you're being charged with a major crime, a Grand Jury needs to review the evidence and agree that there is sufficient cause to indict you. The Grand Jury originated as an English common law concept that was used both in England and the Colonies. An interesting side fact is that today the United States and Liberia are the only countries in the world that still have Grand Juries.

Also, Grand Juries are used only to secure indictments in cases involving civilians. The United States military doesn't need to have a Grand Jury hearing to indict military personnel. You voluntarily forego some of your constitutional rights by joining the U.S. armed forces.

In writing the opinion for the Supreme Court in *Costello v United States* (1956), Justice Hugo Black explained that the basic purpose of a Grand Jury is "to provide a fair method for instituting criminal proceedings against persons believed to have committed crimes." Justice Black added that a Grand Jury was "convened as a body of laymen, free from technical rules, acting in secret, pledged to indict no one because of prejudice and to free no one because of special favor."

Frank Costello was convicted of income tax evasion. He appealed his conviction on the grounds that he should never have been indicted because only hearsay evidence had been presented to the Grand Jury. Justice Hugo Black explained the Court's refusal to quash the indictment by stating that

> if indictments were to be held open to challenge on the ground that there was inadequate or incompetent evidence before the grand jury, the resulting delay would be great indeed. The result of such a rule would be that, before trial on the merits, a defendant could always insist on a kind of preliminary trial to determine the competency and adequacy of the evidence before the grand jury. This is not required by the Fifth Amendment.

The counterargument is that a district attorney can get a Grand Jury to indict a ham sandwich. Justice Harold Burton, while concurring with the majority decision in *Costello*, expressed just such a concern:

> I assume that this Court would not preclude an examination of grand-jury action to ascertain the existence of bias or prejudice in an indictment. Likewise, it seems to me that, if it is shown that the grand jury had before it no substantial or rationally persuasive evidence upon which to base its indictment, that indictment should be quashed. To hold a person to answer to such an empty indictment for a capital or otherwise infamous federal crime robs the Fifth Amendment of much of its protective value to the private citizen.

Next, "nor shall any person be subject for the same offence to be twice put in jeopardy of life or limb." No double jeopardy. If you've been acquitted, you cannot be re-tried for the same crime. In other words, if you've been busted for a crime and found innocent, they can't try you again for the same crime.

This concept originated in ancient Roman law with the principle *non bis in idem*, which means "not twice against the same." One of the earliest cases involving the Double Jeopardy Clause made it to the Supreme Court in 1889. A man named Nielson was living in Utah with his two wives. He was a Mormon, and at that time, the Mormon Church still accepted polygamy, but it was, and still is, illegal in the United States. Eventually, word that he was living with two women got out, and Nielson was arrested and convicted for illegal cohabitation. He did his time, paid his fine, and then after he was released, he was arrested again, this time for adultery. Nielson, who had already been sentenced to jail and a fine for cohabitation, was now being sentenced to jail and a fine for adultery. He felt cohabitation and adultery were the same, and he was being tried a second time for the same offense. He appealed his conviction.

The Supreme Court ruled that the second trial for the same conduct violated the Double Jeopardy Clause of the Fifth Amendment. The conviction for the crime of unlawful cohabitation was a bar to his subsequent prosecution for the crime of adultery.

In 2024, in deciding *McElrath v Georgia*, the Supreme Court made it crystal clear that an acquittal in a criminal trial absolutely prevents the person acquitted from being tried again for the same offence. Damian McElrath had stabbed his mother to death in 2012. He was tried for murder, and the jury returned a verdict of not guilty by "reason of insanity." He was found "guilty but mentally ill" on two other less serious charges. The Georgia Supreme Court found that the two verdicts were inconsistent, vacated both verdicts, and ordered that McElrath be re-tried on all counts. McElrath appealed arguing that a second trial would violate his Fifth Amendment protections against double jeopardy. The U.S. Supreme Court agreed. The decision was unanimous. Writing for the Court, Justice Ketanji Brown Jackson made the following statement:

> The Double Jeopardy Clause of the Fifth Amendment protects individuals from being tried or punished more than once for the same offense, establishing that a verdict of acquittal is final and prohibits any future prosecution for the same offense. An acquittal includes any decision demonstrating the prosecution's failure to provide sufficient evidence for criminal liability, making such a verdict inviolable and irreversible. This principle is crucial, ensuring the finality and integrity of jury verdicts in protecting defendants' rights.

And this brings us to The Juice: O.J. Simpson: Heisman Trophy winner, star NFL running back, sports commentator, movie actor, and Hertz rent-a-car spokesperson. In October 1995, Simpson was acquitted by a jury on two counts of murder: that of his ex-wife Nicole Brown Simpson and her friend Ronald Goldman. At the time, it was the most widely publicized trial in criminal history. Americans were glued to their TV sets during the eight-month trial. Even foreign leaders were fascinated by the spectacle. It is said that when Boris Yeltsin met President Clinton, he asked him, "Do you think O.J. did it?" An estimated 150 million Americans watched on October 3 when the verdict of not guilty was read in court.

There was DNA evidence indicating Simpson was guilty, but in 1995, DNA evidence was a relatively new thing. His defense team convinced the jury that there was reasonable doubt that the incriminating blood sample had been mishandled by lab scientists and technicians. There were questionable circumstances that surrounded other prosecution exhibits. And, the detective who built the case against Simpson was painted by Simpson's defense attorneys as a racist who had a history of police misconduct and using racial slurs. The accusations probably helped to convince the jury of O.J.'s innocence.

In 2006 a book, *If I did It: Confessions of a Killer*, allegedly written by Simpson and Pablo Fenjves, was about to be published. The authors claimed the book was a fictional account of how, if Simpson was guilty, he had committed the murders. The "if" in the title was made deliberately small—almost too small to read—as if O.J. was admitting "I did it." Which many people suspected he had. Amidst public outcry publication of the book was delayed but it did eventually come out.

Ronald Goldman's family, who eventually wrote the forward to the book, were awarded the publication rights. The title of the book was changed to drop the "if." So, why did the victim's family get the royalties? Because in 1996, the families of the victims filed civil suit against O.J. Simpson for the wrongful deaths of Nicole Brown Simpson and Ronald Goldman. The jury found in favor of the plaintiffs and awarded them 33.5 million dollars in compensatory damages.

If you are wondering how it was that O.J. Simpson who was found not guilty of the murders in criminal court, could be re-tried in civil court and found guilty. The answer is the Double Jeopardy Clause does not apply in civil suits. In a civil case for wrongful death, the plaintiffs had to prove only that the defendant's intentional and unlawful conduct resulted in the victim's death. The burden of proof in the civil case was a preponderance of the evidence—a much lesser burden than is required in a criminal case.

A criminal prosecution involves different laws, a different court system, and different burdens of proof. Specifically, the definition of first-degree murder in the context of the O.J. Simpson case requires that the act be done with malice aforethought and premeditation. To convict in the criminal court, the case against the defendant must be proven beyond a reasonable doubt.

Is the former football hero a murderer? A civil jury found it more likely than not that he caused the death of his ex-wife and Ronald Goldman. A criminal jury, however, was unable to find beyond a reasonable doubt that he had committed first-degree murder. Legally, the outcomes do not contradict each other. And being taken to civil court after you've been acquitted in criminal court does not constitute Double Jeopardy as protected by the Fifth Amendment.

One last part to this story, in 2016, a knife from the original murder scene surfaced in police evidence. Some believe the knife had been "stashed" by a corrupt cop to protect Simpson. But even if that knife shows irrefutably that O.J. committed the crime, it won't change the outcome. He cannot be re-tried criminally for the murders of his ex-wife and Ronald Goldman because it would violate his Fifth Amendment rights.

We are finally to the most famous words in the Fifth Amendment, certainly the part that is invoked in every courtroom drama you've ever watched: "Nor shall be compelled in any criminal case to be a witness against himself." In other words, I plead the Fifth. I'm not answering your question because I don't want to risk incriminating myself. I am not going to tell you anything.

Of course, the problem with taking the Fifth is that it implies that you have something to hide, that you are guilty. Which is why defense attorneys frequently choose not to have their clients take the stand. Because if they do, they will be cross examined by the prosecutor, and if they are caught in a lie, they will be guilty of perjury, which is a felony. During the O.J. Simpson murder trial, there were 150 persons who testified, but O.J. did not take the stand.

When someone pleads the Fifth, that person is invoking the Self-Incrimination Clause. It protects persons accused of committing a crime from being forced to testify against themselves. In the U.S. judicial system, a person is presumed innocent, and it is the responsibility of the prosecution to prove guilt beyond a reasonable doubt. Like other pieces of evidence, once presented, words can be used powerfully against a person. Lawyers and prosecutors are experts at manipulating testimony. The Self-Incrimination Clause protects the accused from having their words used against them.

The right against self-incrimination is rooted in seventeenth-century English common law. Back then, there was a group of Protestants with a different take on Christianity known as the Puritans. The problem was their take on Christianity didn't mesh with the Crown's and sometimes Puritans were coerced or tortured into confessing their religious affiliation. Many chose to remain silent. They wouldn't admit they were Puritans, but they wouldn't lie and say they weren't. They simply refused to self-incriminate. The law in England was changed around the mid-1600s to grant citizens the right against self-incrimination.

Puritans who fled religious persecution brought this idea of not having to answer the prosecutor's questions with them to America, where it would eventually become codified in the Bill of Rights. Today, courts have found the right against self-incrimination to include testimonial or communicative evidence at police interrogations. This is why lawyers often tell their clients to respond, "I do not recall" to any questions if they are not absolutely sure of the answer.

If you aren't as certain of the answer as your name or date of birth, then the best answer is "I do not recall." Because if, for example, you are being interviewed by the FBI and you recall something incorrectly, you could be charged with obstruction of justice and if convicted, sentenced to prison for five years. Former First Lady, Senator and Secretary of State Hillary Clinton understands this. When she was interviewed by the FBI about the information on her private server, she responded that she did not recall 39 times. Not to be outdone by his opponent in the 2016 presidential election, President Donald Trump did not recall the answers to 27 questions posed by Special Counsel Robert Mueller who was investigating Russian interference in the 2016 election and possible obstruction of justice by the President.

What about the defendant like O.J. Simpson who chooses not to testify at his trial. Does not being willing to testify indicate one's guilt? We all know lawyers and prosecutors can twist your words against you, but won't the truth come out? Wouldn't the innocent want to defend themselves? If you were a juror, and you knew the defendant was unwilling to testify or say anything to the police, would you hold that against him?

Let us go back to Los Angeles, California, on December 2, 1961. A woman named Essie Mae Hodson is found in a dumpster outside her apartment complex. She is bleeding and in shock. She dies at the hospital the next day from her injuries. A witness testified that earlier that night, he had seen a man named Edward Griffin trying to force himself on her, and another witness said he saw Griffin coming out of the alley where Hodson had been found, and at the time, he was buttoning up his pants. Edward Griffin was arrested for the rape and murder of Essie Mae Hodson. Since he had multiple felony convictions on his record, he refused to testify at the trial. The prosecutor used that as evidence of Griffin's guilt, and in his closing argument to the jury said, "Essie Mae is dead. She can't tell you her side of the story. The defendant won't." It's a powerful statement for sure.

The judge, in his instructions to the jury, noted that Griffin's failure to testify did not create a presumption of guilt. But then he added:

> As to any evidence or facts against him which the defendant can reasonably be expected to deny or explain because of facts within his knowledge, if he does not testify or if, though he does testify, he fails to deny or explain such evidence, the jury may take that failure into consideration as tending to indicate the truth of such evidence

The jury convicted Griffin, and he was sentenced to death. He appealed, and the Supreme Court in *Griffin v California* (1965) overturned his conviction. Justice William O. Douglas in the opinion for the Court, wrote:

> The same standards must determine whether an accused's silence in either a federal or state proceeding is justified. We take that in its literal sense, and hold that the Fifth Amendment, in its direct application to the Federal Government and in its bearing on the States by reason of the Fourteenth Amendment, forbids either comment by the prosecution on the accused's silence or instructions by the court that such silence is evidence of guilt

No person "shall be compelled in any criminal case to be a witness against himself." In other words, your taking the Fifth and refusing to testify cannot be held against you as a sign of your guilt. Even though the evidence against him was pretty compelling, Griffin walked.

Arguably the most famous Fifth Amendment court case about self-incrimination is *Miranda v Arizona*: a 1966 case that forever changed how arrests are carried out by law enforcement in America. Ernesto Miranda, a Mexican immigrant living in Phoenix Arizona was arrested for the kidnapping and rape of an 18-year-old girl. The victim identified him in a police lineup. Miranda was taken into an interrogation room and questioned by the police for two hours until he finally confessed to the crimes.

During the interrogation, police did not tell Miranda about his Fifth Amendment protection against self-incrimination or for that matter, his Sixth Amendment right to an attorney. The case went to trial in an Arizona state court and the prosecutor used Miranda's confession as evidence. The police even got him to write this statement:

> I do hereby swear that I make this statement voluntarily and of my own free will, with no threats, coercion, or promises of immunity, and with full knowledge of my legal rights, understanding any statement I make may be used against me

Miranda's court-appointed lawyer Alvin Moore objected that Miranda's confession was not truly voluntary and should be excluded. But the judge overruled the objection and Miranda was found guilty, sentenced to 20–30 years for both the crime of rape and kidnap, sentences to serve concurrently.

Miranda appealed and eventually this case ended up in the Supreme Court. Miranda's conviction was overturned because Miranda had not been properly advised of his Fifth Amendment protection against self-incrimination. Miranda got to walk.

Chief Justice Earl Warren, in writing the majority opinion, set the standard for police interrogations:

> He [the suspect] must be warned prior to any questioning that he has the right to remain silent, that anything he says

can be used against him in a court of law, that he has the right to the presence of an attorney, and that, if he cannot afford an attorney one will be appointed for him prior to any questioning if he so desires. Opportunity to exercise these rights must be afforded to him throughout the interrogation. After such warnings have been given, and such opportunity afforded him, the individual may knowingly and intelligently waive these rights and agree to answer questions or make a statement. But unless and until such warnings and waiver are demonstrated by the prosecution at trial, no evidence obtained as a result of interrogation can be used against him.

That led to the Miranda warning, which police customarily read to suspects as they are taken into custody:

You have the right to remain silent. Anything you say or do can and will be held against you in a court of law. You have the right to speak to an attorney. If you cannot afford an attorney, one will be appointed for you. Do you understand these rights as they have been read to you?

If it makes you feel any better Miranda was eventually arrested and convicted of his crimes. Was it Double Jeopardy? No, because the original case was thrown out. In 1967, the prosecution introduced other evidence, including witness testimony, but not Miranda's previous confession. This time, he was convicted and served time. And the Supreme Court denied review. In 1972, Miranda was paroled and, true story, made his living after that autographing police officer's Miranda cards. He was stabbed to death in a bar in 1976.

The Supreme Court decision which let self-confessed kidnapper and rapist Ernesto Miranda go free was not unanimous. Justice Byron White in his dissenting opinion argued that the Fifth Amendment protection against self-incrimination only should apply if the defendant is compelled to testify against his will, and that it should not apply if the defendant voluntarily confesses to a crime even if he was not explicitly advised of his Fifth Amendment rights. He issued the following warning:

> In some unknown number of cases, the Court's rule will return a killer, a rapist or other criminal to the streets and to the environment which produced him, to repeat his crime whenever it pleases him. As a consequence, there will not be a gain, but a loss, in human dignity. The real concern is not the unfortunate consequences of this new decision on the criminal law as an abstract, disembodied series of authoritative proscriptions, but the impact on those who rely on the public authority for protection, and who, without it, can only engage in violent self-help with guns, knives and the help of their neighbors similarly inclined. There is, of course, a saving factor: the next victims are uncertain, unnamed and unrepresented in this case.

The next section of the Fifth Amendment is known as the Due Process Clause: No person shall "be deprived of life, liberty or property without due process of law." It has its roots in thirteenth-century England. The Magna Carta: the Royal Charter King John of England agreed to in 1215 for the protection of people's rights had a due process clause: A 1354 rendition of the Magna Carta contained the following provision: "No man of what state or condition he be, shall be put out of his lands or tenements nor taken, nor disinherited, nor put to death, without he be brought to answer by due process of law."

Dissecting the Due Process Clause in the Fifth Amendment, you'll notice some words come to mind: Person, Life, Liberty. The definitions are important. Person means person, not U.S. citizen. The Supreme Court in *Zadvydas v Davis* (2001) ruled that the Due Process Clause applies to non-citizens who are within the United States—no matter whether their presence is "unlawful, involuntary or transitory." If you're on U.S. soil, it applies. That includes juveniles. Even children are entitled to a full hearing before their criminal case can be transferred from the juvenile justice system to the adult justice system.

Life—obviously the right to live and be alive. But that doesn't mean you can't be executed for a crime. Indeed, the Supreme Court has ruled that a defendant may be tried for a capital crime and deprived of life as a penalty as long as the proper procedures are followed.

Liberty, which the Supreme Court in *Bolling v Sharpe* (1954) defined as "Liberty, under law, extends to the full range of conduct which the individual is free to pursue and it cannot be restricted except for a proper government objective."

Here's an example of the Due Process Clause in action. In 2001, a man named Yaser Hamdi is captured on the battlefield in Afghanistan. Hamdi was a U.S. citizen, born in Louisiana, but raised in Saudi Arabia. The U.S. Government claims he was fighting with the Taliban against U.S. forces, and he is declared an illegal enemy combatant. He is remanded to the prison at Guantanamo Bay and detained for almost three years without being charged with a crime and with no access to a lawyer.

In June 2002, Hamdi's father filed a petition for a writ of Habeas Corpus: a writ requiring that a person under arrest be brought before a judge or into court, especially to secure the person's release unless lawful grounds are shown for their detention. The question before the courts was did the Federal Government have the right to deny Fifth Amendment protections to illegal combatants who were U. S. citizens.

The Supreme Court said no. In *Hamdi v Rumsfeld* (2004), the Court held that Hamdi's Due Process rights were being violated. He was being detained without a charge, without bail, and without access to a lawyer, all of which violated his Fifth Amendment rights. The Court agreed that U.S. citizens may be held as enemy combatants, but they still were entitled to the protections afforded by the Fifth Amendment. Justice Sandra Day O'Connor wrote the majority opinion for the Court. In it, she noted that

> an interrogation by one's captor, however effective an intelligence-gathering tool, hardly constitutes a constitutionally adequate fact-finding before a neutral decision-maker.

In other words, even though what the Government was doing at Guantanamo Bay—holding people without bond and questioning them—may have been in the best interest of the American intelligence apparatus, if they were U.S. citizens, it was a violation of their Fifth Amendment right to Due Process, and therefore illegal.

Justice O'Connor added:

> It is during our most challenging and uncertain moments that our nation's commitment to due process is most severely tested; and it is in those times that we must preserve our commitment at home to the principles for which we fight abroad.

It is a powerful statement; an important reminder that there is no point in fighting for the American way, to preserve our values, if we aren't exercising them ourselves. As the German philosopher Friedrich Nietzsche reminds us, "Whoever fights monsters should see to it that in the process he does not become a monster." That's what the Supreme Court was trying to say when it came to how the United States was treating enemy combatants. Even when it's hard, even when it's not in our country's best interests, we must uphold our most sacred values. One of which is due process for the accused, even when the accused are our nation's enemies.

The final clause of the Fifth Amendment prevents the Government from taking private property "for public use, without just compensation." Basically, the government can take your land, but they can't do it without compensating you. Governments at every level in the United States—Federal, State, County, City can acquire private property using eminent domain: the right of a government or its agent to expropriate private property for public use, with payment of compensation. The presumption is the government needs the property for the greater good.

In 1893, the United States Congress authorized the Secretary of War to acquire the land on which the 1863 Battle of Gettysburg had been fought in order to preserve it as a National Military Park. The Company that owned the land sued the Federal Government on the grounds that the seizing of their property violated their Fifth Amendment rights.

The Supreme Court in *United States v Gettysburg Electric Railway Company* (1896) ruled that if the railroad company was paid fair market value for the land, the acquisition was lawful. In terms of public use, Justice Rufus W. Peckham, on behalf of the majority wrote, "No narrow view of the character of this proposed use should be taken. Its national character and importance, we think, are plain." In other words, since the Government has a legitimate purpose to take the land as long as it compensates the owner at a fair price, the Government has the right to do so.

The simple truth is that the Courts almost always side with the Federal, State, County, or City Government in eminent domain cases. The decisions are not always popular, but, perhaps Mr. Spock from Star Trek best articulated the Government's view when he said, "The needs of the many outweigh the needs of the few, or the one."

The Fifth Amendment: sometimes controversial, yet incredibly important.

The Sixth Amendment:
The Right to a Speedy Public Jury Trial

The Sixth Amendment dictates that in a criminal prosecution, the accused is entitled to be tried by a jury of his peers. It reads:

> In all criminal prosecutions, the accused shall enjoy the right to a speedy and public trial, by an impartial jury of the State and district wherein the crime shall have been committed, which district shall have been previously ascertained by law, and to be informed of the nature and cause of the accusation; to be confronted with the witnesses against him; to have compulsory process for obtaining witnesses in his favor, and to have the Assistance of Counsel for his defense.

The Sixth Amendment provides the following seven discrete protections:

1. The right to a speedy trial
2. The right to a public trial
3. The right to an impartial jury
4. The right to be informed of pending charges
5. The right to confront and to cross-examine adverse witnesses
6. The right to compel favorable witnesses to testify at trial through the subpoena power of the judiciary
7. The right to legal counsel

These protections are afforded to the accused at the Federal level. Following the adoption of the Fourteenth Amendment, these protections (and the others afforded by the Bill of Rights) were extended to the State level. It doesn't matter who the prosecutor is or in what jurisdiction you are being tried. The Sixth Amendment protections apply because of the Constitution's Supremacy Clause. Article VI, Clause 2 of the Constitution is an unequivocal statement that the Constitution is the Supreme Law of the Land:

> This Constitution, and the Laws of the United States which shall be made in Pursuance thereof; and all Treaties made, or

which shall be made, under the Authority of the United States, shall be the supreme Law of the Land; and the Judges in every State shall be bound thereby, any Thing in the Constitution or Laws of any State to the Contrary notwithstanding.

First thing, the accused is guaranteed the right to a speedy trial. But what is the definition of speedy? A week? A year? In September 1958, Willie Barker and Silas Manning were arrested for murder. They were accused of having beaten an elderly couple to death in Christian County, Kentucky. The State chose to try Manning first. After a series of trials, he was convicted in 1962. Barker was tried and convicted in October 1963, five years after he had first been charged with the crime. Barker claimed his Sixth Amendment right to a speedy trial had been violated by the length of time that had elapsed from the moment he had been arrested to the start of his trial.

In 1972, the Supreme Court in *Barker v Wingo* ruled that Barker had waived his right to a speedy trial because he had waited three and one-half years before objecting to the delay, and that the delay had not unduly prejudiced his right to a fair trial. Justice Lewis Powell in writing the opinion for a unanimous Court laid down a four-part case-by-case test for determining whether the defendant's speedy trial right has been violated.

> A balancing test necessarily compels courts to approach speedy trial cases on an *ad hoc* basis. We can do little more than identify some of the factors which courts should assess in determining whether a particular defendant has been deprived of his right. Though some might express them in different ways, we identify four such factors: length of delay, the reason for the delay, the defendant's assertion of his right, and prejudice to the defendant.

One of the more interesting cases involving the right to a speedy trial is *Doggett v United States* (1992). In February 1980, Mark Doggett was indicted for drug trafficking. At the time, Doggett was in Panama. The DEA agent in charge of the investigation discovered in September 1981 that Doggett was serving time in a Panamanian prison on drug charges. He asked the Panamanian authorities to return Doggett to the United States after he had completed his sentence. But Doggett was released without the DEA being notified. In September 1982, he returned to the United States, where he behaved as a model citizen, earning a college degree, getting married, and holding a steady job until, in September 1988, eight and a half years after he had been indicted, Doggett was arrested, pleaded guilty, and was convicted. Doggett appealed his conviction on the grounds that he had been denied a speedy trial due to the Government's negligence in failing to arrest him earlier than it did. The Court agreed that he "would have faced trial 6 years earlier than he did but for the Government's inexcusable oversights." His conviction was overturned and Doggett went free.

In the opinion for the Court in *Doggett*, Justice David Souter noted the dangers of ignoring the Sixth Amendment's speedy trial protections:

> We have observed in prior cases that unreasonable delay between formal accusation and trial threatens to produce more than one sort of harm, including "oppressive pretrial incarceration," "anxiety and concern of the accused," and "the possibility that the [accused's] defense will be impaired" by dimming memories and loss of exculpatory evidence....Of these forms of prejudice, "the most serious is the last, because the inability of a defendant adequately to prepare his case skews the fairness of the entire system."

In all criminal prosecutions, the Sixth Amendment guarantees that the accused shall enjoy the right not just to a speedy trial, but to a public one. Trials usually are open to the public, but the right to a public trial is not absolute. In cases where excess publicity would serve to undermine the defendant's right to due process, in high-profile cases, or where the evidence being presented includes sensitive or classified information, limitations can be put on public access to the proceedings. Examples of cases involving closure issues include organized crime cases (overall security concerns), rape cases (decency concerns), and cases involving juveniles.

The accused may also request a closure of the trial; though, it must be demonstrated that there is a substantial probability that the defendant's right to a fair trial will be prejudiced by publicity that closure would prevent.

The requirement that judicial proceedings be public includes pretrial hearings, motions and *voir dire*, the process by which jurors are selected. In *Press-Enterprise Company v Superior Court* (1984), the Supreme Court concluded that barring the press from attending the jury selection proceedings, and later refusing to release the transcript of the *voir dire* proceedings violated the Sixth Amendment rights of the press and through it the public. As Chief Justice Warren Burger explained:

> The presumption of openness may be overcome only by an overriding interest based on findings that closure is essential to preserve higher values, and is narrowly tailored to serve that interest. The interest is to be articulated along with findings specific enough that a reviewing court can determine whether the closure order was properly entered.

The right to a trial by jury has always depended on the nature of the offense with which the defendant is being charged. Petty offenses, misdemeanors—those punishable by imprisonment for no more than six months—are not covered by the jury requirement. Also, in the United States, except for serious offenses (such as murder), minors are usually tried in a juvenile court, which limits the sentence allowed, but forfeits the right to a jury.

In criminal trials, twelve-person juries are the norm. That is always the case in Federal prosecutions, but in 1970, in *Williams v Florida*, the Supreme Court concluded that a jury of six members did not violate a defendant's Sixth Amendment rights. In the opinion for the Court, Justice Byron White briefly reviewed the history of trial by jury:

> That history revealed a long tradition attaching great importance to the concept of relying on a body of one's peers to determine guilt or innocence as a safeguard against arbitrary law enforcement. That same history, however, affords little insight into the considerations that gradually led the size of that body to be generally fixed at 12. Some have suggested that the number 12 was fixed upon simply because that was the number of the presentment jury from the hundred, from which the petit jury developed. Other, less circular but more fanciful reasons for the number 12 have been given, "but they were all brought forward after the number was fixed," and rest on little more than mystical or superstitious insights into the significance of "12."

In 1978, in *Ballew v Georgia*, the Court ruled that a Georgia law providing for five-person juries was unconstitutional, thereby making six the constitutionally acceptable minimum number of jurors in certain criminal trials.

The film, *12 Angry Men,* is a classic courtroom drama portraying the deliberations of jurors trying to reach a unanimous verdict. In criminal cases, the verdict must be unanimous. But that wasn't always the case. In fact, in Louisiana up until 2019, a 10 to 2 majority could still pass a guilty verdict. Enter Evangelisto Ramos. In 2016, he had been found guilty of second-degree murder, and sentenced to life in prison without the possibility of parole. A Louisiana jury had voted 10 to 2 to convict him.

Ramos read up on the law books that were in the prison library, and appealed on the grounds that the 10 to 2 decision to convict him was a violation of his Sixth Amendment rights. The case ended up where it often does in the lap of the Supreme Court as *Ramos v Louisiana* (2020). In the opinion for the Court, Justice Neil Gorsuch referred back to English common law in explaining the Court's decision that jury verdicts in criminal trials needed to be unanimous:

> The requirement of juror unanimity emerged in 14th- century England and was soon accepted as a vital right protected by the common law. As Blackstone explained, no person could be found guilty of a serious crime unless "the truth of every accusation ... should ... be confirmed by the unanimous suffrage of twelve of his equals and neighbors, indifferently chosen, and superior to all suspicion." A " 'verdict, taken from eleven, was no verdict' " at all.

The Supreme Court sided with Ramos. His guilty verdict was reversed. And even though there was DNA evidence against him, he got to walk. In a 6–3 decision, the Court ruled that the Sixth Amendment mandates a unanimous verdict in all federal and state criminal jury trials.

The assumption is that if 12 impartial jurors, people who don't know you, have no inherent bias against you simply by virtue of your race, ethnicity, gender, or other characteristics, and have not been influenced by media coverage, listen to the prosecution and defense's cases and after that believe you are guilty, well then, you are. The issue is, how do you find impartial jurors? How do you find people that are unbiased?

In 2017, a Mexican American named Miguel Angel Pena-Rodriguez was standing trial in Colorado. He was accused of sexually assaulting two teenage girls in a restroom. Pena-Rodriquez was found guilty of unlawful sexual contact and harassment, but something didn't sit right with two of the jurors on the jury. After the jury was discharged, the two jurors, who felt they had been pressured to vote Guilty, went to speak with the Pena-Rodriguez's defense council, and told them that one of the other 12 jurors they served with seemed to hold some pretty appalling views. Apparently during deliberation, he had said, "Mexican men had a bravado that caused them to believe they could do whatever they wanted with women" and "Nine times out of ten Mexican men were guilty of being aggressive toward women." He also said the defendant's alibi witness was not credible because the witness was in the United States illegally.

Jurors are prohibited from discussing the deliberations that occurred in the jury room. This is known as the no impeachment rule, and its purpose is to prevent a juror from trying to discredit a verdict. However, in the case of *Pena-Rodriguez v Colorado* (2017), the Supreme Court in a 5–3 decision decided to overturn Pena-Rodriguez's conviction. As Justice Anthony Kennedy explained in the majority opinion:

> The Nation must continue to make strides to overcome race-based discrimination. The progress that has already been made underlies the Court's insistence that blatant racial prejudice is antithetical to the functioning of the jury system and must be confronted in egregious cases like this one despite the general bar of the no-impeachment rule.

A jury must be impartial! Not having an impartial jury is a violation of the Sixth Amendment, but it is not always easy to empanel an impartial jury. This is even more so in today's 24/7 news media and social media world where pundits and influencers opine seemingly around the clock, well before the jury is selected and the trial begins. Finding jurors who have not been exposed to the media onslaught is nearly impossible in high-profile cases even when there is a change in venue. Selecting jurors who have not been influenced by the media coverage can be a defense attorney's nightmare during *voir dire*.

On Christmas Day, 1843, the home of George Houseman, an oysterman who was away at sea, burned to the ground. It was arson, but it was also murder since the burnt remains of his wife and daughter showed signs of blunt force trauma. Houseman's sister, Polly Bodine, was accused of committing the crimes. The media had a field day. The details of the murders were recounted in lurid detail. Rumors about Bodine—she had abortions committed adultery, had committed other murders, and even drank gin—were printed in the newspapers.

Edgar Allen Poe, Walt Whitman, and P.T. Barnum all weighed in on the story. Bodine's first trial on Staten Island ended in a mistrial. All attempts to conduct a second trial there failed because it was not possible to empanel an unbiased jury. Bodine was then tried in Manhattan and found guilty, but the Supreme Court threw out the conviction on the grounds that Bodine, who was being referred to in the press as a witch, could not have gotten a fair trial in New York City because of the publicity.

The venue was changed to Newburgh, NY, where Bodine was tried again, and this time acquitted. In 1846, a change in venue could make it possible to select 12 unbiased jurors, but is that still possible in today's Internet-connected world?

Imagine, you're on trial. Do you want women on the jury or men? Perhaps you think women will be more sympathetic? But what if you're accused of sex crimes against women? We all have inherent biases, and these biases may influence us when we judge other people's potential bias. Which is why the jury selection process is called *voir dire*, from the French for "speak the truth." This is when the judge, defense lawyers, and prosecutors ask jurors questions and try to pack their 12 picks into the jury box. Which begs the question, if you were on trial, who would you want in your jury box?

In 1972, a man named Billy Taylor was charged with using a butcher's knife to kidnap, rape, and rob a woman. He was indicted by a grand jury in St. Tammany Parish, Louisiana, was tried by an all-male jury, and convicted of aggravated kidnapping. As required by Louisiana law at that time, he was sentenced to death. The reason there were no women jurors in Taylor's trial is because the State Constitution of Louisiana specified that "it would be a special hardship for each and every woman to perform jury service." Women were not to be called for jury duty because "society cannot spare any women from their present duties."

In other words, women had women's work to do, and that did not include jury duty. In Louisiana at the time, if a woman wanted to serve on a jury, she needed to request in writing that she be added to the pool of eligible jurors. Which explains why Billy Taylor was convicted by an all-male jury, and why he appealed his conviction on the grounds that he had not been tried by an impartial jury of his peers.

The Supreme Court in *Taylor v Louisiana* (1975) agreed with Taylor, overturned his conviction, and ordered Louisiana to re-try him. The Court also overturned Louisiana's jury selection system as an unconstitutional violation of the Sixth Amendment. Justice Byron White in the opinion for the Court stated:

> The issue we have, therefore, is whether a jury selection system which operates to exclude from jury service an identifiable class of citizens constituting 53% of eligible jurors in the community comports with the Sixth and Fourteenth Amendments.

The Court's answer was no it did not: The "selection of a...jury from a representative cross section of the community is an essential component of the Sixth Amendment right to a jury trial." White went on to say that excluding women from juries deprived defendants of the "commonsense judgment of the community" that juries were designed to impart.

The Sixth Amendment guarantees an impartial jury, but that jury cannot be drawn from anywhere. It must come from the jurisdiction where the crime took place. The accused has to be tried in "the state and district wherein the crime shall have been committed." That's known as the Vicinage Clause, the provision in the Sixth Amendment regulating the vicinity from which a jury pool is to be selected. Vicinage, of course, is derived from the French word, *voisinage*, meaning neighborhood. You can't fly your jurors in from New York if you're trying someone in Virginia. Jury selection must be from the State or Federal district where the alleged crime took place.

The Accusation Clause of the Sixth Amendment provides that in all criminal prosecutions, the accused shall enjoy the right to be "informed of the nature and cause of the accusation." This means that when you are arrested, officers of the law must inform you of the crime or crimes you are accused of committing. They can't just arrest you and hold you until they figure it out.

The Confrontation Clause provides that in all criminal prosecutions the accused shall have the right to be "confronted with the witnesses against him." This means not only do you know what you are being accused of, you have the chance to confront the people accusing you. Usually this takes place in the form of cross-examinations during a trial.

In August 1985, John Coy was arrested and charged with sexually assaulting two 13 year-old girls. At his trial, the girls were permitted to testify from behind a screen so they would not have to look at him. Coy appealed his conviction on the grounds that his Sixth Amendment right to confront adverse witnesses had been violated. The Iowa Supreme Court took the position that since Coy's attorney could cross-examine the girls, even though they were behind a screen, his Confrontation Clause right had not been impinged, and upheld the conviction.

The Supreme Court, in *Coy v Ohio* (1988), sided with Coy and overturned his conviction. The Court in a 6–2 decision held that:

> The Confrontation Clause, by its words, provides a criminal defendant the right to "confront" face-to-face the witnesses giving evidence against him at trial. That core guarantee serves the general perception that confrontation is essential to fairness, and helps to ensure the integrity of the factfinding process by making it more difficult for witnesses to lie.

In addition to having the right to confront the prosecution's witnesses face-to-face, the Compulsory Process Clause of the Sixth Amendment gives the accused the right to call witnesses to testify on his behalf. The accused shall enjoy the right to have "compulsory process for obtaining witnesses in his favor." If any witness refuses to testify, that person may be compelled to do so by the court or face legal action—fine or even in rare cases imprisonment—for failing to honor a subpoena.

Finally, the Sixth Amendment includes the right of the accused to have "the assistance of counsel for his defense." This means you have the right to have your lawyer present during police interrogations, and from the start of judicial proceedings right through the trial and appeal process.

Clarence Earl Gideon was not known for making smart life choices. He was a man with an eighth-grade education who ran away from home when he was in middle school. He spent much of his early adult life as a drifter, spending time in and out of prisons for nonviolent crimes. On June 3, 1961, Gideon was living in Panama City, Florida. That day, a witness told the police that he had seen Gideon leaving the Bay Harbor Pool Room at 5:30 in the morning carrying a bottle of wine and a bottle of Coca-Cola. The poolroom had been robbed sometime after midnight; the cigarette machine had been smashed open, and money was taken from the cash register.

Gideon was arrested for breaking into a poolroom, charged with felony breaking and entering, convicted, and sentenced to five years in prison. At the start of his trial, Gideon told the judge that he could not afford to hire an attorney, and asked the judge to appoint one to represent him. The judge replied:

> Mr. Gideon, I am sorry, but I cannot appoint Counsel to represent you in this case. Under the laws of the State of Florida, the only time the Court can appoint Counsel to represent a Defendant is when that person is charged with a capital offense. I am sorry, but I will have to deny your request to appoint Counsel to defend you in this case."

Gideon replied, "The United States Supreme Court says I am entitled to be represented by counsel." But the court denied his request, and Gideon had to represent himself for his defense. Abraham Lincoln famously said that "the man who represents himself has a fool for a client."

In prison, using what he had learned from the law books in the prison library, and with the help of a fellow inmate who had a legal background, Gideon applied for a writ of *habeas corpus* to the Florida

Supreme Court, which denied his request, and then to the United States Supreme Court. The term *habeas corpus* is Latin for "you have the body." Courts can use a writ of *habeas corpus* to determine if the incarceration of a prisoner is valid.

Gideon's petition, in which he claimed that the trial court had violated his constitutional rights when it refused to appoint an attorney to defend him, was handwritten in pencil on a single sheet of paper. The Supreme Court took the case, and the first thing the Court did was appoint an attorney to represent him. In *Gideon v Wainwright* (1963), the Court unanimously held that "the right of an indigent defendant in a criminal trial to have the assistance of counsel is a fundamental right essential to a fair trial." In the opinion for the Court Justice Hugo Black noted that "lawyers in criminal courts are necessities, not luxuries."

The Court reasoned that the right to counsel was "fundamental" and must be provided by the government if the defendant cannot afford to hire their own. Clarence Gideon was re-tried, and acquitted.

The consequences of the *Gideon* decision were far-reaching. Not only were defendants now guaranteed their constitutional right to counsel, but state and local jurisdictions realized that they needed to follow the Supreme Court's mandate. So, the decision in this case led to the creation of public defender offices where there previously had been none, and the expansion of the relatively few that were in existence at that time. This is why today if you are arrested in any state, and can't afford a lawyer, one will be provided for you.

Gideon's petition to the Supreme Court, the document, handwritten by a man with an eighth-grade education, that ensured the Sixth Amendment right to counsel to all on U.S. soil, is on display at the Rubenstein Gallery at the National Archives.

Inherent in the Sixth Amendment's right to counsel is the right to the effective assistance of counsel. The litmus test for determining whether the legal assistance provided to a defendant was ineffective is whether assistance by a better lawyer would have resulted in a different judgment. In *Strickland v Washington* (1984), Sandra Day

O'Connor laid down a two-part test for determining if the defendant had received ineffective legal assistance.

> A convicted defendant's claim that counsel's assistance was so defective as to require reversal of a conviction or setting aside of a death sentence requires that the defendant show, first, that counsel's performance was deficient and, second, that the deficient performance prejudiced the defense so as to deprive the defendant of a fair trial.

The case involved David Leroy Washington, a Florida man who had pled guilty to three capital murder charges. He was sentenced to death. He appealed his sentence, arguing that he would not have been sentenced to death, but for the fact that his attorney had failed to provide the effective assistance guaranteed by the Sixth Amendment.

In her opinion, Justice O'Connor made it clear that overturning a conviction on the basis of ineffective legal assistance was no easy matter:

> Judicial scrutiny of counsel's performance must be highly deferential, and a fair assessment of attorney performance requires that every effort be made to eliminate the distorting effects of hindsight, to reconstruct the circumstances of counsel's challenged conduct, and to evaluate the conduct from counsel's perspective at the time. A court must indulge a strong presumption that counsel's conduct falls within the wide range of reasonable professional assistance.

The Court ruled that David Leroy Washington had not been denied effective counsel. Two months after the Court handed down its decision, he was executed for his crimes.

The Sixth Amendment: the array of protections in criminal proceedings for which all Americans should be grateful.

The Seventh Amendment:
The Jury has the Last Word in a Civil Suit

The Seventh Amendment basically extends the protections afforded by the Sixth Amendment in criminal prosecutions to civil suits. It reads:

> In Suits at common law, where the value in controversy shall exceed twenty dollars, the right of trial by jury shall be preserved, and no fact tried by a jury, shall be otherwise re-examined in any Court of the United States, than according to the rules of the common law.

The Seventh Amendment has a Preservation Clause which preserves the right to trial by jury, and a Reexamination Clause which prevents judges and appellate courts from overriding a jury's verdict.

The Seventh Amendment's Preservation Clause requires jury trials in all cases for which they had been required under English common law. In a series of rulings, the Supreme Court has concluded that a jury of at least six persons is required in a civil trial, and that jury trials are not required in cases involving maritime law, suits against the Federal Government, and some patent disputes. Juries are also not required when the parties agreed to waive the right to a jury trial.

The first case involving the Seventh Amendment to come before the Supreme Court was *United States v Wonson* (1812), a case in which the losing party in a federal district court moved to have the case re-tried in a circuit court. Justice Joseph Story denied the motion for a new trial. He ruled that the historical precedent for the Seventh Amendment was English common law:

> Beyond all question, the common law here alluded to is not the common law of any individual state (for it probably differs in all), but it is the common law of England, the grand reservoir of all our jurisprudence.

Under English common law, a motion for a new trial could only be "granted in the discretion of the court, before which the suit is depending, for good cause shown; or unless the judgment of such court is reversed by a superior tribunal, on a writ of error." Justice Story concluded that an appeals court was able to examine "general errors of law" but that it could never "re-try the issues already settled by a jury."

Justice Willis Devanter in writing the majority opinion for the Supreme Court in *Slocum v New York Insurance Company* (1913) referred back to *Wonson* in explaining the Court's decision to order a new trial. In this case, the jury had found in favor of the plaintiff, but the circuit court of appeals reversed the jury's verdict, and found in favor of the defendant. "In other words, the circuit court of appeals directed a judgment for one party when the verdict was for the other." Devanter went on to explain that the circuit court's action was in violation of English common law, and thus, of the Seventh Amendment:

> The jury, taking the law as given by the court, apply that law to the facts as they find them to be, and express their conclusions in the verdict. The power of the court to grant a new trial if, in its judgment, the jury have misinterpreted the instructions as to the rules of law or misapplied them is unquestioned.

The Reexamination Clause of the Seventh Amendment, derived as it is from English common law, precludes a judge or an appellate court from directing a verdict. The court can only order a new trial. But Devanter added that a new trial is not necessarily a bad thing.

> As is said in Blackstone's Commentaries, vol. 3, p. 391: "A new trial is a rehearing of the cause before another jury....The parties come better informed, the counsel better prepared, the law is more fully understood, the judge is more master of the subject, and nothing is now tried but the real merits of the case."

So, what constitutes a civil suit worthy of having its day in court? Twenty bucks. The value of whatever is in question must exceed 20 dollars. This is interesting because in 1791, 20 dollars meant a lot more than it does today. The average annual wage in the U.S. in 1791 was 65 dollars. When the Seventh Amendment was ratified, 20 dollars could have purchased 20 acres of land. I think we can safely say that James Madison wasn't thinking about inflation, or civil suits involving judgments in the millions of dollars when he wrote the Seventh Amendment.

The Amendment has not been updated. Civil suits in the U.S. can be for as little as 20 bucks, and still have a jury because of the Seventh Amendment's protections. Frankly, it would cost the state more to pay the jurors than the suit is worth. But no one today is suing for 20 dollars.

The National Center for State Courts has a Civil Litigation Cost Model, which as of 2013 reported that the median costs for litigation ranged from $43,000 to $122,000 depending on the type of case. A 2008 survey revealed that attorney's regularly turn down cases with median estimated costs of under $100,000 because they do not feel it would be cost-effective for them to litigate. These exorbitant costs can prevent cases from being filed or force cases to settle that should go to trial. No rational person could be expected to be willing to incur such legal fees unless the expected return (monies awarded to the plaintiff or monies saved by the defendant) greatly exceeded the costs.

Of course, the Framers could not predict how large civil suits would be in the future, or what they would be for. Civil suits can include breach of contract claims, disputes over property ownership, and between landlords and tenants, medical malpractice and accidental injury claims, and marital disputes.

A tort is a civil wrong for which the offender is legally liable. While a single individual can bring a wrongful death or injury suit, the largest civil settlement to-date was in 1998, when the four major tobacco companies agreed to settle the suit that had been brought by the attorney generals of 46 states. The companies agreed to pay $206 billion to the states to reduce the costs of treating the smoking-related illnesses of Medicaid recipients.

People file civil suits for a great many reasons. In 2019, Syed Husain filed a civil suit in Los Angeles County Superior Court against his ex-girlfriend, Elina Todorov. According to the complaint, "Over the course of their 14-year relationship, plaintiff spent hundreds of thousands of dollars on defendant. He would frequently purchase for defendant fancy meals, airline tickets, luxury hotel accommodations, fine jewelry, designer handbags, high-end clothing, and more." Husain was asking for $225,000 in damages for "intentional infliction of emotional distress." A Los Angeles judge called his claim "ridiculous."

When it comes to matters of the heart, each state tends to view matters differently. California has an "anti-heart balm" statute which prevents litigation involving romantic entanglements. In 1994, California's Fourth District Court of Appeals concluded in *Askew v Askew* that "the statute obviously prohibited (and still prohibits) lawsuits seeking contract damages for the emotional pain of a broken engagement."

In North Carolina, on the other hand, in 2010, Cynthia Shackelford claimed her husband's alleged mistress, Anne Lundquist, had broken up her marriage, and sued her for "alienation of affection." The jury awarded her $5 million in compensatory damages and $4 million in punitive damages. A high price to pay for having sex with another woman's husband. But the Seventh Amendment's Preservation and Reexamination Clauses guarantee that in all civil suits, the jury will have the last word.

The right to a jury trial in civil suits was reaffirmed in June, 2024. The Supreme Court in *Securities and Exchange Commission v Jerkesy et al.* ruled in a 6–3 decision that the SEC's practice of using in house tribunals to exact fines from companies for alleged securities violations violated the accused's Seventh Amendment right to a trial by jury. Up until Jerkesy, the enforcement actions of the Securities and Exchange Commission were very lucrative. For fiscal year 2024 (October 1, 2023 through September 30, 2024) the SEC had filed 583 enforcement actions and obtained $8.2 billion in fines. The haul was enough to make any criminal organization envious.

The Eighth Amendment:
Cruel and Unusual Punishments

The Eighth Amendment protects those convicted of committing crimes from being subjected to cruel and unusual punishments. It reads:

> Excessive bail shall not be required, nor excessive fines imposed, nor cruel and unusual punishments inflicted.

So, "Excessive bail shall not be required." Seems a bit ambiguous. I mean, what is excessive? The lack of clarity in using the word "excessive" is deliberate. Why? Because it ensures the government can protect the public from flight risks and criminals who may recidivate while awaiting trial. In other words, whatever works. Setting bail must serve the government's interests.

Excessive bail is bail that is set at a figure higher than an amount reasonably calculated to ensure the asserted governmental interest. Usually, that interest is to guarantee that the accused will stand trial. If the bail set by the court is greater than the amount that would ensure that interest, then the bail is excessive, and the defendant's attorney may petition the court for a reduction of the amount. If the court fails to grant the request, the attorney may immediately appeal to a higher court.

The highest amount for bail ever set was for Texas real estate heir and accused murderer Robert Durst. In 2003, he was arrested in Galveston and bail was set at three billion dollars. Durst had a history of jumping bail. When he had been arrested on a previous charge in 2001, bail was set at $250,000. He paid and ran. A warrant for his arrest was issued for jumping bail, and the police finally caught up with him while he was shoplifting a chicken salad sandwich at a Wegmans in Bethlehem, Pennsylvania. So, knowing that he had previously posted and skipped on $250,000 dollars bail, the question is was setting bail at three billion excessive?

The Fourteenth Court of Appeals in Galveston thought so. Justice Wanda Fowler wrote in the majority decision: "These amounts were so excessive, no one could meet them, not Durst and not any of the bail companies. This is an example of bail being used as an instrument of oppression." Durst's bail was dropped to $450,000. He was also required to pay for round-the-clock police supervision, and he had to surrender his passport.

Durst was suspected of having been involved in the unsolved 1982 disappearance of his wife. In 2003, he was tried and acquitted for the 2001 murder of his neighbor, Morris Black. The jury in Galveston bought Durst's claim that he had shot Black in self-defense, and apparently did not hold the fact that he had dismembered the victim's body and disposed of it in the ocean against him. In 2015, Durst appeared in the HBO miniseries, "The Jinx: The Life and Deaths of Robert Durst." While wearing a hot mike, he appeared to confess to three murders, that of his wife, his neighbor, and his friend, Susan Berman who was killed in 2000. The "Jinx" brought to light new evidence that led to Durst, in 2021, being tried for Berman's murder. He was found guilty and sentenced to life imprisonment. Durst was sentenced on October 14, 2021; he died in prison three months later on January 22, 2022. The wheels of justice sometimes turn very slowly indeed.

There are some suspects who are not given bail. Sometimes they are just flight risks. More often, they are repeat violent offenders. Anthony Salerno, better known as Fat Tony was the underboss of the Genovese crime family in New York. He was arrested in 1985, and along with eight other New York bosses, indicted in what became known as the Mafia Commission Trial. All of them were denied bail. Fat Tony appealed and eventually the case ended up in the Supreme Court. In *United States v Salerno* (1987), the Court found that Salerno could be held without bail because of his potential danger to the community. Salerno was convicted on RICO charges and sentenced to 100 years. He died in prison in 1992.

The Supreme Court has granted government prosecutors wide latitude not just in recommending the amount of bail a court should set, but whether instead of setting bail, the court should hold the defendant in pretrial detention. For example, when, as in the case involving Salerno, the government contends that if released the defendant would be likely to intimidate witnesses. As Chief Justice

William Rehnquist wrote in the majority opinion, "The bail clause was lifted with slight changes from the English Bill of Rights Act. In England, that clause has never been thought to accord a right to bail in all cases, but merely to provide that bail shall not be excessive in those cases where it is proper to grant bail."

The Eighth Amendment also requires that excessive fines shall not be imposed. The Supreme Court first addressed the question of what constitutes an excessive fine in *United States v Bajakajian* (1998). Hosep Bajakajian was caught at Los Angeles International Airport trying to leave the country without having declared that he had more than $10,000 in his possession. The government sought forfeiture of the entire amount, $357,144, that he had on his person at the time he was apprehended. The question before the Court was: Was the amount the government wanted forfeited "disproportionate to the gravity of defendant's offense." The Court concluded it was. In the majority opinion, Justice Clarence Thomas wrote:

> The touchstone of the constitutional inquiry under the Excessive Fines Clause is the principle of proportionality: The amount of the forfeiture must bear some relationship to the gravity of the offense that it is designed to punish.

In 2012, Tysons Timbs received a sizable sum of money from his father's life insurance when his dad passed. He used $42,000 of that money to purchase a land rover. Unfortunately, he used the rest of it to purchase drugs, and in 2013, he was arrested for selling an undercover cop $225 worth of drugs. Timbs pleaded guilty and was sentenced to a year of house arrest and a fine of $1,200 which he paid. But then because of Indiana's forfeiture law, the state confiscated Timbs' land rover saying he had used it to transport drugs.

Timbs appealed and the case, now backed by the Institute of Justice, ended up at the Supreme Court in *Timbs v Indiana* (2019). Timbs' lawyers argued that seizure of the vehicle made it virtually impossible for him to work and thus constituted an excessive fine. Justice Ruth Bader Ginsburg, in the majority opinion for the Court, hearkened back to the Magna Carta in discussing what constitutes an excessive fine:

> The Excessive Fines Clause traces its venerable lineage back to at least 1215, when Magna Carta guaranteed that "[a] Free-man shall not be amerced for a small fault, but after the manner of the fault; and for a great fault after the greatness thereof, saving to him his contenement....As relevant here, Magna Carta required that economic sanctions "be proportioned to the wrong" and "not be so large as to deprive [an offender] of his livelihood."

Justice Ginsburg went on to point out that:

> For good reason, the protection against excessive fines has been a constant shield throughout Anglo-American history: Exorbitant tolls undermine other constitutional liberties. Excessive fines can be used, for example, to retaliate against or chill the speech of political enemies.... Even absent a political motive, fines may be employed "in a measure out of accord with the penal goals of retribution and deterrence," for "fines are a source of revenue," while other forms of punishment "cost a State money."

The Supreme Court ruled in favor of Timbs. Seizing an asset that prevents one from working, especially after the person has already served time and paid a fine, is excessive.

Alright, the last and most famous part of the Eighth Amendment: "nor cruel and unusual punishments inflicted." Now that doesn't mean punishments can't be severe. What it really means is the punishment must fit the crime. This part of the Eighth Amendment has its origin, like so much of our Bill of Rights, in the Magna Carta:

> A free man shall not be fined for a small offense unless according to the measure of the offense and for a great offense he shall be fined according to the greatness of the offense.

As used in the Magna Carta, the word "fined" included the entire gamut of punishments up to and including the death penalty. The Eighth Amendment does not specifically say this, but we can infer it from the language. In the United States, and in most of the world, people tend to believe in retributive justice. The theory is that when someone breaks the law justice requires that the offender suffer in return, and that the response to a crime be proportional to the offence. Clearly the concept of proportional justice, and even what constitutes cruel and unusual punishment has changed throughout history.

The stocks were a common form of punishment in 1700s America. So were hangings. And I won't even get into the brutality of the tortures and executions that went on in England. But, thanks to the Eighth Amendment, that has all changed. And thanks in some part to a man named Paul Weems.

Weems was a U.S. citizen living in the Philippines in the early 1900s. At that time, the Philippines was an American colony, ceded to the United States by the Spanish at the end of the Spanish American War. Weems was a disbursing officer for the Bureau of Coast Guard and Transportation. He was charged with falsifying an official document for the purpose of defrauding the government. Weems was convicted in a Philippine court. Under a territorial law inherited from the Spanish penal code, Weems was sentenced to *cadena temporal*: 15 years of hard labor in chains. Weems appealed on the grounds that 15 years of breaking rocks while chained up was a cruel and unusual punishment for falsifying a document.

The case eventually ended up in the Supreme Court because of the Supremacy Clause. The one that states that no law can be in violation of the Constitution, which is the Supreme Law of the land. Well, it may have been a Philippine court that sentenced Weems, but the Philippines was an American colony, and the Supreme Court had the final word.

In *Weems v United States* (1910), the Court determined that the sentence of 15 years in prison for the offense that Weems had committed was unconstitutionally cruel and unusual. The conditions of Weems' incarceration specifically included being chained from wrist to ankle and compelled to work at "hard and painful labor." Justice Joseph McKenna, in the opinion for the Court, stated that so severe a penalty for such a relatively minor crime was "repugnant to the Bill of Rights."

The Court ordered the judgment reversed, with directions to dismiss the charges entirely. Weems was set free. But this brings up an interesting question. We have modern chain gangs. Flogging was the usual punishment for breaches of military discipline, especially on naval vessels. We used to put petty thieves in the stocks. And we execute criminals. So, what is cruel and unusual?

In some countries, amputation of a limb is the sentence for certain serious crimes. Would you rather lose a hand or be given a lethal injection? Isn't executing someone the most cruel and unusual punishment of all?

In 1976, the Supreme Court heard the appeal of Troy Greg. He had been convicted of armed robbery and murder, and a Georgia jury had decided that he should be executed for his crimes. In *Gregg v Georgia*, the Court in a 7–2 decision reached the following conclusion: "We now hold that the punishment of death does not invariably violate the Constitution."

Four years earlier, in 1972, the Supreme Court had heard the appeal of William Furman, a Georgia man who had been arrested, tried, convicted, and sentenced to death for murder. Furman had been trying to rob someone's house in the middle of the night. He thought the homeowner was asleep, but unfortunately, he woke up. Furman claimed he had tried to run away, but he tripped and fell, which caused the gun he was carrying to go off, accidentally killing the homeowner. Furman was found guilty of murder and sentenced to death. He appealed on the grounds that the death penalty was a cruel and unusual punishment given that it was an accident, not the intention of his crime, which was burglary.

The case, *Furman v Georgia*, went to the Supreme Court and in 5–4 decision Furman's sentence was commuted to life in prison. The Court's primary holding was that "the death penalty is unconstitutional under the Eighth Amendment prohibition against cruel and unusual punishment when it is imposed in an arbitrary and capricious manner that leads to discriminatory results."

Each of the five concurring justices issued a separate opinion. Justices Thurgood Marshall and William Brennan took the position that the death penalty was unconstitutional. As Justice Brennan explained:

> Death is an unusually severe and degrading punishment; there is a strong probability that it is inflicted arbitrarily; its rejection by contemporary society is virtually total; and there is no reason to believe that it serves any penal purpose more effectively than the less severe punishment of imprisonment. The function of these principles is to enable a court to determine whether a punishment comports with human dignity. Death, quite simply, does not.

Justice Potter Stewart also recognized the finality of the death sentence:

> The penalty of death differs from all other forms of criminal punishment, not in degree, but in kind. It is unique in its total irrevocability. It is unique in its rejection of rehabilitation of the convict as a basic purpose of criminal justice. And it is unique, finally, in its absolute renunciation of all that is embodied in our concept of humanity.

Stewart chose not to address the question of "whether capital punishment is unconstitutional for all crimes and under all circumstances."

> The instinct for retribution is part of the nature of man, and channeling that instinct in the administration of criminal justice serves an important purpose in promoting the stability of a society governed by law. When people begin to believe that organized society is unwilling or unable to impose upon

criminal offenders the punishment they "deserve," then there are sown the seeds of anarchy – of self-help, vigilante justice, and lynch law.

Stewart articulated the consensus of the five concurring justices when he wrote:

> These death sentences are cruel and unusual in the same way that being struck by lightning is cruel and unusual. For, of all the people convicted of rapes and murders in 1967 and 1968, many just as reprehensible as these, the petitioners are among a capriciously selected random handful upon whom the sentence of death has in fact been imposed.

In other words, not everyone was getting the death penalty for the same crimes. Stewart went on to say:

> I simply conclude that the Eighth amendment cannot tolerate the infliction of a sentence of death under legal systems that permit this unique penalty to be so wantonly and so freakishly imposed.

Based on the *Furman* decision, a moratorium was declared on the death penalty. During the next four years, 37 states enacted new death penalty laws intended to overcome the Supreme Court's concerns about the arbitrary imposition of the death penalty. Standards were created to guide the discretion of juries and judges in imposing death sentences.

In 1976, the United States started executing criminals again, starting in Georgia with the lethal injection of murderer Marion Wilson. His last meal apparently was a thin crust pizza, 20 buffalo wings, one pint of butter pecan ice cream, some apple pie, and grape juice.

Murderers could now be executed, but what about other heinous crimes. Should we only execute for capital crimes, such as murder, rape, and treason? The Supreme Court has not ruled on whether the death penalty is still acceptable punishment for crimes against the government such as espionage and treason. The last time anyone was executed in the United States for that crime was in 1953, when Julius and Ethel Rosenberg were electrocuted for passing nuclear secrets to Soviet agents. But the Court has decided whether it is permissible to execute rapists. In 2003, Patrick Kennedy was sentenced to death for the brutal rape of his eight-year-old stepdaughter. Did Kennedy deserve to die? That was the question facing the Supreme Court in *Kennedy v Louisiana* (2008).

In a 5–4 decision, the Court held that "the Eighth Amendment bars states from imposing the death penalty for the rape of a child where the crime did not result, and was not intended to result, in the child's death." Patrick Kennedy may have been a terrible person, but death was a cruel and unusual punishment for his crime because no one had died. In the opinion for the Court, Justice Anthony Kennedy quoted from the decision in *Coker v Georgia* (1977) in which the Court overturned a death penalty conviction for the rape of an adult woman as justification to extend the Court's judgment to cases involving the rape of a child.

> Rape is without doubt deserving of serious punishment; but in terms of moral depravity and of the injury to the person and to the public, it does not compare with murder, which does involve the unjustified taking of human life. Although it may be accompanied by another crime, rape by definition does not include the death of ... another person. The murderer kills; the rapist, if no more than that, does not.... We have the abiding conviction that the death penalty, which 'is unique in its severity and irrevocability... is an excessive penalty for the rapist who, as such, does not take human life.

Not everyone agreed with this decision which was handed down during a presidential election season. Then candidate Barak Obama said:

> I have said repeatedly that I think that the death penalty should be applied in very narrow circumstances for the most egregious

of crimes ... I think that the rape of a small child, six or eight years old, is a heinous crime and if a state makes a decision that under narrow, limited, well-defined circumstances the death penalty is at least potentially applicable, that that does not violate our Constitution.

His opponent, John McCain, also felt the Court had gotten it wrong, "That there is a judge anywhere in America who does not believe that the rape of a child represents the most heinous of crimes, which is deserving of the most serious of punishments, is profoundly disturbing."

Justice Samuel Alito was one of the four dissenting justices in *Kennedy*. He wrote:

> The Court today holds that the Eighth Amendment categorically prohibits the imposition of the death penalty for the crime of raping a child. This is so, according to the Court, no matter how young the child, no matter how many times the child is raped, no matter how many children the perpetrator rapes, no matter how sadistic the crime, no matter how much physical or psychological trauma is inflicted, and no matter how heinous the perpetrator's prior criminal record may be. The Court provides two reasons for this sweeping conclusion: First, the Court claims to have identified "a national consensus" that the death penalty is never acceptable for the rape of a child; second, the Court concludes, based on its "independent judgment," that imposing the death penalty for child rape is inconsistent with " 'the evolving standards of decency that mark the progress of a maturing society.' ".... Because neither of these justifications is sound, I respectfully dissent.

What about the way in which you are allowed to execute someone? Clearly, we no longer draw and quarter or behead people. But in 2020, a man was electrocuted in Tennessee. Ten years earlier, in 2010, a man had been executed by a firing squad in Utah. No one has been executed by hanging in the United States since 1996, but that is still not all that long ago. And that's the thing, cruel and unusual is defined somewhat ambiguously by the current culture.

In 1755, it was okay to burn someone at the stake. But that was the last time it happened on U.S. soil. Today, Americans would certainly find burning someone an unacceptable method of execution. Yet, the assumption is that the majority of Americans still find lethal injection, hanging, the firing squad, and the electric chair to be justifiable punishments.

Lethal injection has become the standard form of capital punishment that is practiced today. But in 2019, two inmates on death row in Tennessee requested that they be put to death by electrocution rather than by lethal injection. It turns out that lethal injections may be a crueler and more unusual punishment than initially thought. According to several autopsy reports, many death row inmates who were executed with lethal injection suffered pulmonary edema as they died. Their lungs filled with blood and plasma, they felt paralyzed and breathless, and they experienced the feeling of suffocation or drowning as they died.

Which brings us back to the original question: What is cruel and unusual? Executions don't always go smoothly. This is why Anne Boleyn famously said, "I heard say the executioner was very good, and I have a little neck." She wanted to make sure she was beheaded with one definitive swing. Nobody wants their execution to get botched and end up dying in horrible pain.

But that does happen, even today. Imagine it from the perspective of Clayton Lockett. He had been convicted of murder, rape, and kidnapping, and sentenced to death. On April 29, 2014, he was scheduled to be executed by lethal injection at the Oklahoma State Penitentiary in McAlester, Oklahoma. Multiple attempts were made first by a paramedic and then by the attending physician to insert the IV needle first into Lockett's left arm, then into the brachial vein in his biceps, the jugular vein in his neck, and the subclavian vein adjacent to his collar bone, all without success. The IV was finally inserted into Lockett's femoral vein in his groin.

Once the IV needle was inserted, midazolam, a sedative was administered. Once Lockett was unconscious, the next two drugs, the paralytic agent vecuronium bromide, and the lethal poison, the heart-stopping potassium chloride were inserted into his vein. But Lockett didn't die. He woke up and started to struggle. The execution was then halted, but Lockett died anyway, from a heart attack. It had taken 43 agonizingly painful minutes for him to die.

No one faced charges for Lockett's botched execution. His family filed civil suit but a judge dismissed the case ruling Lockett's prolonged agonizing death was an isolated mishap. But should we care if Clayton Lockett suffered a painful death? Did he care when he kidnapped, raped, and murdered Stephanie Neiman? Did that young woman not also suffer a painful death?

The choice to adopt arguably more humane means of capital punishment has not been the direct result of a decision from the Supreme Court. In fact, the Court has never weighed in on the method of execution chosen by the federal government or by any individual state. The Framers came from a time before lethal injection, and when the stocks were still considered reasonable punishment. But they knew torture was wrong, and they adopted the Eighth Amendment to protect the convicted from cruel and unusual punishments.

In an ideal world, punishment would serve as rehabilitation as well as justice for the victim and protection for society. But of course, we do not live in a perfect world. Prisoners are incarcerated but they still have access to food, exercise, and medical services. Those having committed too heinous a crime to be forgiven are executed, but in a way believed to be humane. Interestingly, Michigan is the only state that has never executed anyone. The last execution under Michigan law occurred in 1830 when Michigan was still a territory. Since Michigan became a state, it has been execution free. Is Michigan the way of the future? One day, will we look back on capital punishment, even when carried out as humanely as possible, as barbaric, antiquated, and as cruel and unusual as being drawn and quartered. Will we one day conclude that Justice Stephen Breyer was correct when he wrote, "I believe it highly likely that the death penalty violates the Eighth Amendment."

The Eighth Amendment protects us from the imposition of excessive bail and excessive fines. It also protects us from the infliction of cruel and unusual punishments. Defining what those are is still an open question. But perhaps Justice Sonia Sotomayor expressed it best:

> By protecting even those convicted of heinous crimes, the Eighth Amendment reaffirms the duty of the government to respect the dignity of all persons.

CHAPTER 4

THIS AND NO MORE: THE NINTH AND TENTH AMENDMENTS

The Ninth and Tenth Amendments limit the powers of the Federal Government to only those delegated to it in the Constitution, and provide that powers not specifically enumerated in the Constitution are reserved for the individual states and/or the American people.

**The Ninth Amendment:
Rights Retained by the People**

The Ninth Amendment reads:

> The enumeration in the Constitution, of certain rights, shall not be construed to deny or disparage others retained by the people.

The Bill of Rights couldn't possibly cover everything. The representatives and senators of the first United States Congress recognized that they probably had left some things out—things that could come up in the future. They were concerned that future generations might argue that because a certain right was not listed in the Bill of Rights, it did not exist. Or, it could be denied to the American people.

Certain rights in the Constitution—the ones that are specifically spelled out—are enumerated rights. The first eight amendments list enumerated rights, from freedom of religion to protection against cruel and unusual punishments. The Ninth Amendment covers the rights not specifically mentioned in the Constitution and the first eight amendments. In essence, just because it isn't in the Constitution doesn't mean it isn't a right.

The right to interstate travel and to apply for a passport are examples of unenumerated rights. It's assumed we have the right to travel both within the country and internationally, but it's not specifically stated anywhere in the Constitution. While travel isn't controversial, in 1965, contraception was. C. Lee Burton, a gynecologist at Yale's Medical School and Estelle Griswold, who headed Planned Parenthood in Connecticut, were convicted of violating the state's 1879 law that made it a crime to use "any drug, medicinal article or instrument for the purpose of preventing conception."

In *Griswold v Connecticut*, the Supreme Court addressed the question, "Does the Constitution protect the right of marital privacy against state restrictions on a couple's ability to be counseled in the use of contraceptives?" By a 7–2 decision, the Court ruled that it did. Justice William O. Douglas in writing the opinion for the Court noted that "specific guarantees in the Bill of Rights have penumbras, formed by emanations from those guarantees that help give them life and substance.... Various guarantees create zones of privacy." He cited the First, Third, Fourth, Fifth, and Ninth Amendments in explaining the Court's decision to declare Connecticut's contraception ban unconstitutional.

In a concurring opinion, Justice Arthur Goldberg argued that any other conclusion would have been a violation of the Ninth Amendment.

> The language and history of the Ninth Amendment reveal that the Framers of the Constitution believed that there are additional fundamental rights, protected from governmental infringement, which exist alongside those fundamental rights specifically mentioned in the first eight constitutional amendments.... [A] judicial construction that this fundamental right is not protected by the Constitution

because it is not mentioned in explicit terms by one of the first eight amendments or elsewhere in the Constitution would violate the Ninth Amendment.

What about abortion? Is the right to terminate a pregnancy an unenumerated right protected by the Ninth Amendment? In 1969, a woman named Norma McCovey was pregnant with her third child—a child that she didn't want to have. She was twenty-one years old and using drugs. She had given her previous two children up for adoption. But this time, she didn't want to carry her child to term.

The problem was, Norma lived in Texas and in 1969 abortion was illegal there except when necessary to save a mother's life. Although Norma's friend, perhaps not realizing that, came up with a different reason Norma could use to justify getting an abortion. She went to the police and claimed she had been raped. Norma's lie was not believed. There was no evidence and the police dropped the case.

Norma then tried to get a back-alley abortion, an illegal one. But the clinic she went to had been shut down by the authorities. Out of options, she finally came across attorneys Linda Coffee and Sarah Weddington. Two lawyers who were looking for pregnant women who were seeking abortions, and they took Norma's case. The U.S. District Court for the Northern District of Texas overturned the Texas law banning abortions. The Court ruled that the Ninth and Fourteenth Amendments guarantee the "the right of choice over events which, by their character and consequences, bear in a fundamental manner on the privacy of individuals."

Texas appealed the decision, and the case went to the Supreme Court. By the way Norma McCovey was her real name, but you probably know her better by the pseudonym she used in court, Jane Roe. We are talking about one of the most controversial cases in Supreme Court history, *Roe v Wade* (1973).

The question before the Court was, does the Constitution protect a woman's right to choose to have an abortion? Written before safe, medically induced abortion as we know it today existed, the

Constitution makes no mention of abortion. It also doesn't mention the right to have children, but that's a pretty obvious one. Well then wouldn't the opposite be true? Wouldn't a woman also have the right not to have children, even if she was already pregnant?

The Supreme Court said yes, she did. In a 7–2 decision, the Court ruled that a pregnant woman's right to choose whether or not to have an abortion is constitutionally protected. In the opinion for the Court, Justice Harry Blackmun wrote:

> This right of privacy, whether it be founded in the Fourteenth Amendment's concept of personal liberty and restrictions upon state action, as we feel it is, or, as the District Court determined, in the Ninth Amendment's reservation of rights to the people, is broad enough to encompass a woman's decision whether or not to terminate her pregnancy.

Blackmun went on to point out that while the right of personal privacy included the decision to have an abortion, that "right is not unqualified, and must be considered against important state interests in regulation."

> A State may properly assert important interests in safeguarding health, in maintaining medical standards, and in protecting potential life. At some point in pregnancy, these respective interests become sufficiently compelling to sustain regulation of the factors that govern the abortion decision. The privacy right involved, therefore, cannot be said to be absolute.

The final ruling of the Court provided an absolute right to privacy in only the first trimester of pregnancy:

> a. For the stage prior to approximately the end of the first trimester, the abortion decision and its effectuation must be left to the medical judgment of the pregnant woman's attending physician.

b. For the stage subsequent to approximately the end of the first trimester, the State, in promoting its interest in the health of the mother, may, if it chooses, regulate the abortion procedure in ways that are reasonably related to maternal health.

c. For the stage subsequent to viability, the State in promoting its interest in the potentiality of human life may, if it chooses, regulate, and even proscribe, abortion except where it is necessary, in appropriate medical judgment, for the preservation of the life or health of the mother.

Justice Byron White wrote a blistering dissent that foreshadowed the Court's decision to overturn both *Roe* and the Court's 1992 decision in *Planned Parenthood of Southeastern Pennsylvania v Casey*, which invalidated state abortion regulations that imposed an "undue burden," that is, a "substantial obstacle in the path of a woman seeking an abortion before the fetus attains viability." White wrote:

> With all due respect, I dissent. I find nothing in the language or history of the Constitution to support the Court's judgment. The Court simply fashions and announces a new constitutional right for pregnant mothers... and, with scarcely any reason or authority for its action, invests that right with sufficient substance to override most existing state abortion statutes. The upshot is that the people and the legislatures of the 50 States are constitutionally disentitled to weigh the relative importance of the continued existence and development of the fetus, on the one hand, against a spectrum of possible impacts on the mother, on the other hand. As an exercise of raw judicial power, the Court perhaps has authority to do what it does today; but in my view its judgment is an improvident and extravagant exercise of the power of judicial review that the Constitution extends to this Court.

White added:

> In a sensitive area such as this, involving as it does issues over which reasonable men may easily and heatedly differ, I cannot accept the Court's exercise of its clear power of choice by interposing a constitutional barrier to state efforts to protect human life and by investing mothers and doctors with the constitutionally protected right to exterminate it. This issue, for the most part, should be left with the people and to the political processes the people have devised to govern their affairs.

Twenty years after the Court handed down its decision in *Casey*, in *Dobbs v Jackson Women's Health Organization* (2022), the Court came to the conclusion that Justice White had expressed in his dissent in *Roe*, and overturned both *Roe* and Casey. Writing for the majority, Justice Samuel Alito began by pointing out that the matter before the Court was highly controversial:

> Abortion presents a profound moral issue on which Americans hold sharply conflicting views. Some believe fervently that a human person comes into being at conception and that abortion ends an innocent life. Others feel just as strongly that any regulation of abortion invades a woman's right to control her own body and prevents women from achieving full equality. Still others in a third group think that abortion should be allowed under some but not all circumstances, and those within this group hold a variety of views about the particular restrictions that should be imposed.

Alito then went on to state the majority opinion:

> We hold that *Roe* and *Casey* must be overruled. The Constitution makes no reference to abortion, and no such right is implicitly protected by any constitutional provision... It is time to heed the Constitution and return the issue of abortion to the people's elected representatives.

Alito also cited a sentence from Justice Antonin Scalia's opinion in *Casey*: "The permissibility of abortion, and the limitations, upon it, are to be resolved like most important questions in our democracy: by citizens trying to persuade one another and then voting." And Alito concluded: "That is what the Constitution and the rule of law demand."

The Ninth Amendment states that "the enumeration in the Constitution, of certain rights, shall not be construed to deny or disparage others retained by the people." But what those unenumerated rights are and who, Congress, the state legislatures, the courts, or the people through ballot initiatives, determines what they are is still subject to debate.

The Tenth Amendment: Rights Retained by the States

The Ninth Amendment deals with unenumerated rights. The Tenth Amendment addresses unenumerated powers. It reads:

> The powers not delegated to the United States by the Constitution, nor prohibited by it to the States, are reserved to the States respectively, or to the people.

Was the intent of the Tenth Amendment such that if a specific power, such as the power to raise taxes, regulate interstate commerce or declare war, was not specified in the Constitution, then that power was reserved to the states or the people? Chief Justice John Marshall didn't think so. Writing the opinion for a unanimous Supreme Court in *McCulloch v Maryland* (1819), a case in which the Court ruled that the State of Maryland could not levy taxes on the Second Bank of the United States, he stated:

> Among the enumerated powers, we do not find that of establishing a bank or creating a corporation. But there is no phrase in the instrument which... excludes incidental or implied powers and which requires that everything granted shall be expressly and minutely described. Even the 10th Amendment omits the word "expressly," and declares only that the powers "not delegated to the United States, nor prohibited to the States, are reserved to the States or to the people," thus leaving the question whether the particular power which may become the subject of contest has been delegated to the one Government, or prohibited to the other, to depend on a fair construction of the whole instrument.

In 1918, Congress passed the Migratory Bird Treaty Act in order to enforce the provisions of a treaty with Canada to protect migrating birds. Missouri objected. The state argued that the Constitution didn't make any reference to limiting the hunting of migratory birds and therefore the Bird Treaty Act was in violation of the Tenth Amendment. The Supreme Court respectfully disagreed.

In a 7–2 decision, the Court, in *State of Missouri v Holland* (1920) held that the Treaty did not violate the Tenth Amendment, and that by virtue of Clause 2 or Article VI of the Constitution (the Supremacy Clause) treaties were the law of the land.

James Madison, even though he wrote the Tenth Amendment, considered it "superfluous" and "unnecessary." In *United States v Darby Lumber Company* (1941), a unanimous Supreme Court agreed with Madison when it held that the Fair Labor Standards Act of 1938 was constitutional, and that the Tenth Amendment could not be used as a basis to prevent the federal government from regulating conditions of employment. Writing for the Court, Chief Justice Harlan Stone made the following observation:

> The [Tenth] amendment states but a truism that all is retained which has not been surrendered. There is nothing in the history of its adoption to suggest that it was more than declaratory of the relationship between the national and state governments as it had been established by the Constitution before the amendment, or that its purpose was other than to allay fears that the new national government might seek to exercise powers not granted, and that the states might not be able to exercise fully their reserved powers.

In *Garcia v the San Antonio Metropolitan Transit Authority* (1985), the Supreme Court in a 5–4 decision upheld the extension by Congress of the Fair Labor Standards Act to state and local government employees. Justice Lewis Powell in his dissent argued that the Court was ignoring "the integral role of the Tenth Amendment in our constitutional theory." He took the position that "judicial enforcement of the Tenth Amendment is essential to maintaining the federal system so carefully designed by the Framers and adopted in the Constitution." Powell went on to explain that his position was in line with what the Framers had intended:

> The Framers had definite ideas about the nature of the Constitution's division of authority between the Federal and State Governments. In The Federalist No. 39, for example, Madison explained this division by drawing a series of contrasts between the attributes of a "national" government and those of the government to be established by the Constitution. While a national form of government would possess an "indefinite supremacy over all persons and things," the form of government contemplated by the Constitution instead consisted of "local or municipal authorities [which] form distinct and independent portions of the supremacy, no more subject within their respective spheres to the general authority, than the general authority is subject to them, within its own sphere"....Under the Constitution, the sphere of the proposed government extended to jurisdiction of "certain enumerated objects only, ... leaving] to the several States a residuary and inviolable sovereignty over all other objects."

In two 5–4 decisions, *United States v Lopez* (1995) and *Printz v United States* (1997), the Supreme Court revisited the Tenth Amendment, ruling in the first case that the Gun-Free School Zones Act of 1990 was unconstitutional because it was an overreach of the Commerce Clause, and in the second case that the interim provision of the Brady Bill that required local law enforcement to conduct background checks on prospective purchasers of hand guns could not be justified by relying on the Necessary and Proper Clause of Article I of the Constitution. In his concurring opinion in *Printz*, Justice Clarence Thomas succinctly stated the opinion of the majority:

> I join the Court's opinion in full, I write separately to emphasize that the Tenth Amendment affirms the undeniable notion that under our Constitution, the Federal Government is one of enumerated, hence limited, powers.

Federalism. Powers not granted to the U.S. National Government are reserved to the States or to the people. What about rights like sports betting? Should the Federal Government determine whether sports betting should be legal, or should that decision be left up to the individual states?

In 1992, Congress passed the Professional and Amateur Sports Protection Act with the intention of ending sports gambling in the United States. The law stated that states may not "sponsor, operate, advertise, promote, license, or authorize by law or compact" sports gambling. The rationale for this was that sports betting was a national problem. As the Senate Judiciary Subcommittee, which held public hearings on the proposed legislation reported: "The harms sports gambling inflicts are felt beyond the borders of those States that sanction it." And that's the really important part. If issues caused by gambling go beyond a state's borders, then it's a federal problem. Or is it?

In 2011, New Jersey held a referendum, a vote for all New Jersey-ites on whether to create a state constitutional amendment that would permit sports gambling. The citizens of New Jersey voted overwhelmingly to legalize sports betting. It was estimated that the federal prohibition against sports betting was going to cost the state approximately $600 million annually in lost revenues. New Jersey filed suit claiming the Professional and Amateur Sports Protection Act violated the Tenth Amendment.

In *Murphy v National Collegiate Athletic Association* (2018), the Supreme Court in a 6-3 decision agreed with New Jersey that the Act violated the Tenth Amendment. In the opinion for the Court, Justice Samuel Alito wrote:

> The legislative powers granted to Congress are sizable, but they are not unlimited. The Constitution confers on Congress not plenary legislative power but only certain enumerated powers. Therefore, all other legislative power is reserved for the States, as the Tenth Amendment confirms. And conspicuously absent from the list of powers given to Congress is the power to issue direct orders to the governments of the States.

The anticommandeering doctrine simply represents the recognition of this limit on congressional authority.

Congress has vast powers but the Tenth Amendment prevents it from commandeering unenumerated powers that rightfully belong to the states. Does *Murphy* set the precedent for other situations in which states choose to ignore federal statutes?

In the United States, the use and possession of cannabis is illegal under federal law for any purpose, by way of the Controlled Substances Act of 1970. And yet a number of states are ignoring the federal law. At the state level, policies regarding the medical and recreational use of cannabis vary greatly, but state laws that permit its use are in conflict with federal law. Cities that offer sanctuary to unauthorized immigrants (persons who are living in the United States illegally) are in violation of federal immigration enforcement statutes. So, who gets to choose, the States or the Federal Government?

Here it is again, the Tenth Amendment, the one that ensures federalism, the separation of powers between Federal and State Government: "The powers not delegated to the United States by the Constitution, nor prohibited by it to the States are reserved to the States respectively, or to the people." Interesting side fact, that last four words of the Amendment—"or to the people"—were handwritten by the clerk of the Senate as the Bill of Rights circulated between the two Houses of Congress.

Handwritten, scribbled in there. It was an afterthought, to once again reaffirm that whatever powers the Federal and State Governments didn't retain, the people did. And isn't that a beautiful way to wrap up the Bill of Rights. After all, the purpose of the Bill of Rights—first and foremost—was to guarantee civil rights and individual liberties to the people and protect them from an oppressive government.

In 2013, there was an essay contest for high school students in the United States. The topic was "Why is the Bill of Rights important?"

Maria Heiselman of Mason High School in Mason, Ohio took third place, but what she wrote was perfect:

> When you think about it, how incredible is it that the Founding Fathers wrote such comprehensive rights that would still be applicable on a daily basis over 200 years later? These rights give each of us the privilege to live a life that is free from fear, oppression, uncertainty, and discrimination. A Bill of Rights was written to protect American citizens from the government. It is this daily protection that enables me to live the American dream sought by our Founding Fathers.

AMENDMENTS ELEVEN TO TWENTY-SEVEN

The first ten amendments, the Bill of Rights, were ratified in 1791. The last amendment to be added to the Constitution was ratified in 1992. During the 201 years that elapsed between the ratification of the Bill of Rights and the ratification of the twenty-seventh amendment, thousands of amendments were proposed, but only seventeen were added to the Constitution. The seventeen amendments that were ratified during those years deal with a wide range of issues. Everything from limiting the scope of the federal judiciary to addressing presidential disability and succession. They provide for equal protection under the law and due process in criminal proceedings. They give Congress the power to levy income taxes, and they give women and eighteen-year-olds the right to vote. These amendments tell the story of the American people's ongoing efforts "to form a more perfect union."

CHAPTER 5

WHAT FEDERAL COURTS CANNOT DO: THE ELEVENTH AMENDMENT

The Eleventh Amendment was ratified on February 7, 1795. It prevents states from being sued by citizens of another state or by non-citizens. It reads:

> The Judicial power of the United States shall not be construed to extend to any suit in law or equity, commenced or prosecuted against one of the United States by Citizens of another State, or by Citizens or Subjects of any Foreign State.

The Eleventh Amendment has its origin in the 1793 Supreme Court decision in *Chisholm v Georgia*. Alexander Chisholm, a south Carolinian, sued the state of Georgia for monies owed to him for goods that he had provided to Georgia during the Revolutionary War. Georgia claimed that the doctrine of sovereign immunity prevented the Supreme Court from hearing the case, and that it could only be sued by someone from out of state if it consented to the suit. Justice James Wilson expressed the question before the Court:

> This is a case of uncommon magnitude. One of the parties to it is a State—certainly respectable, claiming to be sovereign. The question to be determined is whether this State, so respectable, and whose claim soars so high, is amenable to the jurisdiction of the Supreme Court of the United States?

The Court ruled in favor of Chisholm because four of its five members believed that Article 3, Section 2, Clause 2 of the Constitution gave the Court the authority to hear the case. It reads: "In all Cases affecting Ambassadors, other public Ministers and Consuls, and those in which a State shall be Party, the Supreme Court shall have original Jurisdiction."

One member of the Court, Justice James Iredell dissented because he believed that the doctrine of sovereign immunity should have prevented the Supreme Court from hearing the case. In other words, a state could not be sued in federal court without its consent because each state was a sovereign body. His opinion became the law when two years later, in 1795, the Eleventh Amendment was ratified.

In the Federalist Papers: No. 81, Alexander Hamilton had argued that the individual states were sovereign entities and could not be sued without their consent:

> It is inherent in the nature of sovereignty not to be amenable to the suit of an individual **WITHOUT ITS CONSENT**. This is the general sense, and the general practice of mankind; and the exemption, as one of the attributes of sovereignty, is now enjoyed by the government of every State in the Union.

In *Hans v Louisiana* (1890), a case in which a citizen of Louisiana sued the state in federal court for the payment of interest on state-issued bonds that he had purchased, the Supreme Court ruled in favor of Louisiana. In doing so, the Court expanded its interpretation of the Eleventh Amendment to include barring federal courts from hearing suits against a state brought by citizens of that state. As Justice John Marshall Harlan wrote in his concurring opinion: "a suit directly against a state by one of its own citizens is not one to which the judicial power of the United States extends, unless the state itself consents to be sued."

In *Seminole Tribe of Florida v Florida* (1996), the Court in a 5–4 decision ruled that states may not be sued by private parties in federal court without their consent, and that Congress lacks the power to make them, that is to abrogate their sovereign immunity.

Three years later in *Alden v Maine*, the Court again by a 5–4 decision expanded its interpretation of the Eleventh Amendment. A group of probation officers, alleging that the State of Maine had violated provisions of the 1938 Fair Labor Standards Act, sued the state in state court. Both the trial court and the state supreme court dismissed the suit on the grounds that Maine's sovereign immunity prevented it from being sued in its own courts without its consent. The Supreme Court affirmed the judgment of the state courts. In the opinion for the Court, Justice Anthony Kennedy wrote:

> We hold that the powers delegated to Congress under Article I of the United States Constitution do not include the power to subject nonconsenting States to private suits for damages in State Courts, and the State of Maine has not consented to this suit.
>
> Because the Eleventh Amendment makes explicit reference to the State's immunity to private suits, we sometimes refer to the State Sovereign Immunity as "Eleventh Amendment Immunity".
>
> The phrase is a convenient shorthand, but really something of a misnomer, for State Sovereign Immunity neither derives from nor is limited by the terms of the Eleventh Amendment.
>
> ....
>
> Congress has vast power, but not all power.
>
> When Congress legislates in matters affecting the States, it may not treat these sovereign entities as mere prefectures or corporations, Congress must accord States the esteem due to them as joint participants in a federal system.
>
> One beginning with the premise of sovereignty in both the Central Government and the separate States.
>
> Congress has ample means to ensure compliance with valid federal laws but it must respect the sovereignty of the States.

The Eleventh Amendment was added to the Constitution to see that it does.

CHAPTER 6

THE PRESIDENT AND VICE PRESIDENT: THE TWELFTH, TWENTIETH, TWENTY-SECOND, AND TWENTY-FIFTH AMENDMENTS

These amendments address the changes that have been made to the process by which we elect our President and Vice President, limit their term of office, and provide for their succession in the event of a vacancy.

The Twelfth Amendment: Electing the President and Vice President

The Twelfth Amendment was ratified in 1804. It changed the way we elect our President and Vice President from one in which the candidate with the most electoral votes became President and the runner-up became Vice President, to the electoral system we have today in which the winning candidates for president and vice president are from the same political party. It reads:

> The Electors shall meet in their respective states, and vote by ballot for President and Vice-President, one of whom, at least, shall not be an inhabitant of the same state with themselves; they shall name in their ballots the person voted for as President, and in distinct ballots the person voted for as Vice-President, and they shall make distinct lists of all persons voted for as President, and all persons voted for as Vice-President and of the

number of votes for each, which lists they shall sign and certify, and transmit sealed to the seat of the government of the United States, directed to the President of the Senate;

The President of the Senate shall, in the presence of the Senate and House of Representatives, open all the certificates and the votes shall then be counted;

The person having the greatest number of votes for President, shall be the President, if such number be a majority of the whole number of Electors appointed; and if no person have such majority, then from the persons having the highest numbers not exceeding three on the list of those voted for as President, the House of Representatives shall choose immediately, by ballot, the President. But in choosing the President, the votes shall be taken by states, the representation from each state having one vote; a quorum for this purpose shall consist of a member or members from two-thirds of the states, and a majority of all the states shall be necessary to a choice. And if the House of Representatives shall not choose a President whenever the right of choice shall devolve upon them, before the fourth day of March next following, then the Vice-President shall act as President, as in the case of the death or other constitutional disability of the President.

The person having the greatest number of votes as Vice-President, shall be the Vice-President, if such number be a majority of the whole number of Electors appointed, and if no person have a majority, then from the two highest numbers on the list, the Senate shall choose the Vice-President; a quorum for the purpose shall consist of two-thirds of the whole number of Senators, and a majority of the whole number shall be necessary to a choice. But no person constitutionally ineligible to the office of President shall be eligible to that of Vice-President of the United States.

In his September 17, 1796, letter to "Friends and Citizens," his Farewell Address, George Washington had warned his countrymen about the dangers of sectionalism, factionalism, and interference in the domestic affairs of the nation by foreign powers. He wrote that while political parties "may now and then answer popular ends, they are likely in the course of time and things, to become potent engines, by which cunning, ambitious, and unprincipled men will be enabled to subvert the power of the people and to usurp for themselves the reins of government."

In the election of 1796, John Adams received 71 electoral votes; Thomas Jefferson received 68. Four years later, the election of 1800 was contested by candidates from two nascent political parties, the Federalists led by President John Adams and the Democratic-Republicans led by Vice President Thomas Jefferson. The electoral vote count was a tie. Jefferson received 73 votes, but so did his running mate, Aaron Burr. The election was thrown into the House of Representatives, and but for the intervention of Alexander Hamilton on Jefferson's behalf, Burr would have become President. It had taken 36 ballots in the House to elect Jefferson President and Burr Vice President.

The Twelfth Amendment was ratified in time for the election of 1804; its ratification was an acknowledgement that party politics were now an integral part of the electoral process. Going forward electors would cast separate votes for President and Vice President. If no candidate received a majority of the electoral votes, the election would be decided by the House of Representatives with each state casting one vote. If no vice-presidential candidate received a majority, the vice president would be elected by the Senate with each Senator having one vote.

The Twelfth Amendment restricted electors from voting for both a President and a Vice President from the same state in which they resided; only one could be from their state. The Vice President presides over the Senate, and the Amendment made it the Vice President's responsibility to count the electoral votes. Finally, the Twelfth Amendment barred anyone from becoming Vice President who was ineligible to hold the office of President.

In the 2000 presidential election, Vice President Al Gore won the popular vote by a margin of over 500,000, but lost the election to

Governor George W. Bush by 5 electoral votes (271 to 266). In the election of 2016, the popular vote for Hillary Clinton exceeded that for Donald Trump by nearly 3 million, but Trump won the election with a margin of 77 electoral votes.

There are those who argue that the Electoral College is undemocratic, it should be abolished, and instead the President and Vice President should be elected by popular vote. Opponents of direct popular election contend that eliminating the Electoral College would disenfranchise states with smaller populations, and that the people living in large populous states like California, New York, Texas, and Florida would always control the outcome of presidential elections.

Replacing the Electoral College with a direct popular election would require a constitutional amendment, and while Congress might pass one, and the states with large populations might ratify it, the less populous states would not. The Electoral College like the United States Senate serves to ensure the Framers vision of the United States as a republic made up, as we noted in discussing the Eleventh Amendment, of sovereign states.

The Twelfth Amendment's modifications to the electoral process accommodated the development of political parties which have become a quintessential element of the American political system.

The Twentieth Amendment:
The Presidential Inauguration

The Twentieth Amendment, ratified in 1933, did three things. It reduced the time a lame duck President or member of Congress stayed in office by changing the date that a President and Vice President's term ended from March 4 to January 20, and the date the term of a member of Congress ended from March 4 to January 3. It required Congress, by law, to assemble at least once a year at noon on January 3. The Twentieth Amendment also specified who succeeds the President-Elect if he or she dies before Inauguration Day, and what happens if a President-Elect has not been chosen by Inauguration Day. It reads:

> The terms of the President and the Vice President shall end at noon on the 20th day of January, and the terms of Senators and Representatives at noon on the 3d day of January, of the years in which such terms would have ended if this article had not been ratified; and the terms of their successors shall then begin.
>
> The Congress shall assemble at least once in every year, and such meeting shall begin at noon on the 3d day of January, unless they shall by law appoint a different day.
>
> If, at the time fixed for the beginning of the term of the President, the President elect shall have died, the Vice President elect shall become President. If a President shall not have been chosen before the time fixed for the beginning of his term, or if the President elect shall have failed to qualify, then the Vice President elect shall act as President until a President shall have qualified; and the Congress may by law provide for the case wherein neither a President elect nor a Vice President shall have qualified, declaring who shall then act as President, or the manner in which one who is to act shall be selected, and such person shall act accordingly until a President or Vice President shall have qualified.

The Congress may by law provide for the case of the death of any of the persons from whom the House of Representatives may choose a President whenever the right of choice shall have devolved upon them, and for the case of the death of any of the persons from whom the Senate may choose a Vice President whenever the right of choice shall have devolved upon them.

Sections 1 and 2 shall take effect on the 15th day of October following the ratification of this article.

This article shall be inoperative unless it shall have been ratified as an amendment to the Constitution by the legislatures of three-fourths of the several States within seven years from the date of its submission.

In 1845, Congress had passed a law which set the date for presidential elections as the first Tuesday after the first Monday in November, but the presidential term of office did not begin until March 4. Abraham Lincoln, elected in November, could not assume the office of President until March 4, 1861. By which time, South Carolina, Mississippi, Florida, Alabama, Louisiana, and Texas had seceded from the Union. Franklin Delano Roosevelt was elected in the middle of the Great Depression, but he could not begin to address the nation's problems until four months after his election. The Twentieth Amendment shortened the window from election to inauguration from four months to two and one-half months.

Seventeen days before he was to be inaugurated for his first term as president, Franklin Roosevelt was delivering a speech in Miami's Bayfront Park. Giuseppi Zangara, using a pistol he had recently purchased, tried to kill the President-Elect. Anton Cermak, the Mayor of Chicago, who was by Roosevelt's side, was killed, and five bystanders were wounded, but Roosevelt was unharmed.

Zangara missed Roosevelt only because a woman, Mrs. W. F. Cross, the wife of a Miami physician, who was standing next to Zangara saw the gun in his hand. She quickly transferred her purse from her right arm to her left one, so she could grab his arm and divert the bullets. Other than a brief mention in a UPI story, the 5-foot, 4-inch, 100-pound heroine received no acclaim for saving Roosevelt's life.

Had Roosevelt been assassinated, we can assume that the Vice President-Elect, John Nance Garner, would have assumed the office of President. But that was not clearly stated in the Constitution until the Twentieth Amendment was ratified. In addition to dealing with the death of a President-Elect, the Amendment also dealt with a situation in which a President had not been elected by Inauguration Day.

In accordance with the Presidential Succession Act of 1947, if the President dies, is unable to perform the duties of the office, resigns or is removed from office, and there is no Vice President to succeed him or her, then the office devolves upon first, the Speaker of the House, then the President Pro-Tempore of the Senate, and after that members of the Cabinet beginning with the Secretary of State.

An argument can be made that the baton should be passed to members of the Cabinet beginning with the Secretary of State, but while Congress is unlikely to amend the Presidential Succession Act, the Supreme Court may not uphold it. Article 1, Section 6, Clause 2 of the Constitution (the Ineligibility Clause) forbids Members of Congress from holding other federal offices. The Court could rule that Congress exceeded its authority when it inserted the Speaker of the House and the President Pro-Tempore of the Senate into the line of succession, or it could conclude that since the Speaker would resign upon taking the oath of office as President, no Constitutional issues were involved in the succession.

When Congress passed the Twentieth Amendment and sent it to the states for ratification, it set a time limit of seven years. If the Amendment was not ratified within that time frame, then the time allowed for it to be ratified would have expired, and the Amendment could no longer be a candidate for ratification. This was the first time Congress had set a seven-year window for ratification, but it became the standard going forward.

The Twenty-Second Amendment: Presidential Term Limits

The Twenty-Second Amendment establishes presidential term limits. It reads:

> No person shall be elected to the office of the President more than twice, and no person who has held the office of President, or acted as President, for more than two years of a term to which some other person was elected President shall be elected to the office of President more than once. But this Article shall not apply to any person holding the office of President when this Article was proposed by Congress, and shall not prevent any person who may be holding the office of President, or acting as President, during the term within which this Article becomes operative from holding the office of President or acting as President during the remainder of such term.
>
> This article shall be inoperative unless it shall have been ratified as an amendment to the Constitution by the legislatures of three-fourths of the several States within seven years from the date of its submission to the States by the Congress.

George Washington could have been President for life, but he chose to step down after only serving two terms. The American artist, Benjamin West, recalled that when he told King George III that Washington would one day retire and return to private life, "The King said if He did He would be the greatest man in the world."

Washington was succeeded by John Adams, who having lost his bid for reelection to Thomas Jefferson, only served one term. This was the first peaceful transition of power from one political faction, in this case the Federalists, to another, The Democratic-Republicans. It set an important precedent.

Jefferson cemented another, when after serving two terms, he chose to follow Washington's example and retire. Jefferson wrote:

> If some termination to the services of the chief magistrate be not fixed by the Constitution, or supplied by practice, his office, nominally for years, will in fact, become for life; and history shows how easily that degenerates into an inheritance.

The precedent that had been set by Washington and adhered to by Jefferson would be followed by every president until 1940, when Franklin Delano Roosevelt ran for a third term, and won. He ran again in 1944, and won again. On April 12, 1945, 82 days after he was inaugurated for his fourth term, Roosevelt died from a cerebral hemorrhage. His Vice President Harry Truman succeeded him.

Congress concerned with how powerful a popular president could become, passed and sent to the states the Twenty-Second Amendment. It was ratified on February 27, 1951. In addition to setting a two-term limit, the Amendment specifies that a person who succeeds to the office of President and serves as President for more than two years can only be elected to a single term.

Lyndon Johnson succeeded to the office of the President when John F. Kennedy was assassinated on November 22, 1963. He was elected to the office in his own right in 1964. Because he had served as president for less than two years during the term that he had succeeded Kennedy, he could have run for a second term.

Gerald Ford, on the other hand, succeeded Nixon when he resigned on August 9, 1974. Had Ford been elected in his own right in the 1976 presidential election, he would not have been able to run for reelection since he had served more than two years as President during the term that he succeeded Nixon.

Ronald Reagan carried 49 of the 50 states when he was reelected in 1984. He garnered nearly 60% of the popular vote. There is every reason to believe that he might very well have been elected to a third term but for the Twenty-Second Amendment. Reagan believed that the Amendment was "an infringement on the democratic rights of the people."

The argument that is made against the Twenty-Second Amendment is that by placing arbitrary term limits on the office of the President you may be preventing the American people from choosing the person that they want to be President. The counter-argument is that the term limits set by the Twenty-Second Amendment prevent a populist from morphing into a dictator.

The Twenty-Fifth Amendment: Presidential Succession

Ratified on February 10, 1967, the Twenty-Fifth Amendment laid out the steps to be taken to fill vacancies in the office of President and Vice President. It reads:

> In case of the removal of the President from office or of his death or resignation, the Vice President shall become President.
>
> Whenever there is a vacancy in the office of the Vice President, the President shall nominate a Vice President who shall take office upon confirmation by a majority vote of both Houses of Congress.
>
> Whenever the President transmits to the President pro tempore of the Senate and the Speaker of the House of Representatives his written declaration that he is unable to discharge the powers and duties of his office, and until he transmits to them a written declaration to the contrary, such powers and duties shall be discharged by the Vice President as Acting President.
>
> Whenever the Vice President and a majority of either the principal officers of the executive departments or of such other body as Congress may by law provide, transmit to the President pro tempore of the Senate and the Speaker of the House of Representatives their written declaration that the President is unable to discharge the powers and duties of his office, the Vice President shall immediately assume the powers and duties of the office as Acting President.
>
> Thereafter, when the President transmits to the President pro tempore of the Senate and the Speaker of the House of Representatives his written declaration that no inability exists, he shall resume the powers and duties of his office unless the Vice President and a majority of either the principal officers of the executive department or of such other body as Congress may by law provide, transmit within four days to the President pro tempore of the Senate and the Speaker of

the House of Representatives their written declaration that the President is unable to discharge the powers and duties of his office. Thereupon Congress shall decide the issue, assembling within forty-eight hours for that purpose if not in session. If the Congress, within twenty-one days after receipt of the latter written declaration, or, if Congress is not in session, within twenty-one days after Congress is required to assemble, determines by two-thirds vote of both Houses that the President is unable to discharge the powers and duties of his office, the Vice President shall continue to discharge the same as Acting President; otherwise, the President shall resume the powers and duties of his office.

Prior to the ratification of the Twenty-Fifth Amendment, eight presidents had died in office. They were succeeded by their vice presidents. John Tyler was the first Vice President to become President in this way. March 4, 1841, was a cold blustery day in the Nation's Capital, and the newly inaugurated President William Henry Harrison delivered his inaugural address without wearing a coat or a hat. The address was 9,000 words long and must have taken several hours to read. The 68-year-old Harrison caught pneumonia, took to his bed, and died 30 days later. Tyler claimed that he was now the President. Some members of Congress believed that Tyler had only taken up the "powers and duties" of the presidency. However, Tyler's view prevailed and he served as our nation's tenth President, and set the precedent for having the Vice President become President in the event the presidency becomes vacant.

In the morning, on Saturday, July 2, 1881, President James Garfield was at the Baltimore and Potomac Railroad Station in Washington, DC, when he was shot twice by Charles Guiteau. At that time the Republican Party had two factions, the Stalwarts who favored the system of spoils and political patronage, and the Half-Breeds who were for civil service reform. Guiteau was a supporter of the Stalwarts. He said that God had "wanted him to murder Garfield to aid the Stalwarts."

The assassination attempt was successful, but it took Garfield 79 days to die. During which time he was still President. Newspapers reported on his condition daily: "The President was somewhat restless and vomited several times during the early part of the night..." Garfield was a mess, and for over two and a half months, the most powerful person in the land was incoherent and delirious. Clearly, he was incapable of discharging his duties as President. Garfield's Vice President Chester Arthur could do nothing but watch as there was no Constitutional method for him to take power. He was finally sworn in after Garfield died.

Of course, Garfield did not have the nuclear codes. But with the thought that the nation could find itself without a functioning president during the Cold War, and with the Cuban Missile Crisis still fresh on everyone's mind, Congress passed the Twenty-Fifth Amendment on July 6, 1965, and sent it to the states, which only took 18 months to ratify it.

The Twenty-Fifth Amendment explicitly states that upon a president's death, resignation, or removal from office, the Vice President shall become the President. It then provides for filling the office of Vice President by having the President send to Congress the name of the person he or she wants to fill the vacancy. If both houses of Congress by a majority vote, approve of the choice, the nominee becomes the Vice President.

On October 10, 1973, Vice President Spiro Agnew pleaded *nolo contendere* (no contest) in the Federal District Court in Baltimore to one count of income tax evasion. He had been under investigation for bribery, extortion, and income tax evasion during the time he had been the Governor of Maryland. He was fined $10,000 and sentenced to three years of unsupervised probation. Agnew had resigned as Vice President that morning before appearing in court.

President Nixon nominated Congressman Gerald Ford, the House minority leader, for the Office of Vice President on October 12, 1973. It was the first time that the Twenty-Fifth Amendment would be used to fill a vice presidential vacancy. The FBI immediately began a background investigation of Ford, and both the House and

Senate Judiciary committees held hearings on his nomination. The Senate and the House both voted overwhelmingly to confirm Ford's nomination, and on December 6, 1973, he was sworn in as the nation's fortieth Vice President by Chief Justice Warren Burger in front of a joint session of Congress.

Less than a year later, the office of the Vice President is again vacant when following Nixon's resignation in the wake of the Watergate scandal, Vice President Ford is sworn in as the thirty-eighth President of the United States. On August 20, 1974, eleven days after becoming President, Ford nominates the former governor of New York, Nelson Rockefeller, to be his Vice President. Rockefeller's confirmation process takes four months, but he is confirmed and assumes the office of Vice President on December 19, 1974.

If the Twenty-Fifth Amendment is only used to fill vice presidential vacancies, then it serves a valuable purpose. But the Amendment can also serve to let the Vice President serve as the acting President if the President is temporarily unable to perform the duties of the office. On July 13, 1985, President Reagan underwent intestinal surgery to remove a precancerous polyp. Before being anesthetized, he sent a letter to the President Pro Tempore of the Senate and the Speaker of the House transferring the powers of the presidency to Vice President George H. W. Bush, who, in accordance with the Twenty-Fifth Amendment, was for the next eight hours the Acting President of the United States.

The Twenty-Fifth Amendment also provides for the process to be followed in the event that the Vice President and a majority of the members of the Cabinet feel that the President is unable to perform the duties of the office, and the Vice President needs to assume the role of Acting President.

On January 12, 2021, in the aftermath of what happened at the Capitol on January 6, and just eight days before he was to leave office, the House of Representatives on a straight party line vote, approved a resolution calling on Vice President Pence and the members of the Cabinet to invoke the Twenty-Fifth Amendment on the grounds that President Trump was unfit for the office of

President. That same day Vice President Pence wrote a letter to the Speaker of the House, Nancy Pelosi, explaining why he would not honor the House's request:

> With just eight days left in the President's term, you and the Democratic Caucus are demanding that the Cabinet and I invoke the 25th Amendment. I do not believe that such a course of action is in the best interest of our Nation or consistent with our Constitution. Last week, I did not yield to pressure to exert power beyond my constitutional authority to determine the outcome of the election, and I will not now yield to efforts in the House of Representatives to play political games at a time so serious in the life of our Nation.
>
> As you know full well, the 25th Amendment was designed to address Presidential incapacity or disability. Just a few months ago, when you introduced legislation to create a 25th Amendment Commission, you said… "that we must be "[v]ery respectful of not making a judgment on the basis of a comment or behavior that we don't like." Madam Speaker, you were right. Under our Constitution, the 25th Amendment is not a means of punishment or usurpation. Invoking the 25th Amendment in such a manner would set a terrible precedent.

The Twenty-Fifth Amendment establishes the order of and the procedures for presidential and vice-presidential succession. It was never intended to be used as a political expedient.

CHAPTER 7

THE CIVIL WAR AND RECONSTRUCTION, SLAVERY TO CIVIL RIGHTS: THE THIRTEENTH, FOURTEENTH, FIFTEENTH, AND TWENTY-FOURTH AMENDMENTS

The Thirteenth, Fourteenth, and Fifteenth Amendments are known as the Reconstruction Amendments. Ratified in the five years following the end of the Civil War, they abolished slavery, provided guarantees of due process and equal protection under the law, and expanded citizenship and voting rights. The Twenty-Fourth Amendment abolished the poll tax, which had been used by Southern States to deny the voting rights guaranteed by the Fifteenth Amendment.

The Thirteenth Amendment:
Emancipation

In the final days of America's costliest war, the one it fought against itself, Congress sent the Thirteenth Amendment, the one which ended slavery, to President Abraham Lincoln. The Constitution does not provide for the President to have any formal role in the amendment process. And yet the joint resolution for the Thirteenth Amendment was sent to Lincoln for his signature. On February 1, 1865, Lincoln added his signature and, above it, wrote the word "Approved."

The Thirteenth Amendment is the only ratified amendment signed by a President.

Lincoln did not live to see the Amendment ratified. He was assassinated on April 15, 1865, six days after Robert E. Lee had surrendered to Ulysses S. Grant at Appomattox Court House in Virginia, bringing to the end a war in which an estimated 750,000 soldiers (Union and Confederates) and an untold number of civilians, mostly in the South, had died. The Amendment was ratified by twenty-seven of the thirty-six states that had not seceded from the Union, and became the law of the land on December 6, 1865. It reads:

> Neither slavery nor involuntary servitude, except as a punishment for crime whereof the party shall have been duly convicted, shall exist within the United States, or any place subject to their jurisdiction.
>
> Congress shall have power to enforce this article by appropriate legislation.

On January 1, 1863, Lincoln had issued his Emancipation Proclamation which declared "that all persons held as slaves" within the rebellious states "are, and henceforward shall be free." With the stroke of a pen, he had freed four million slaves. But the Proclamation was a wartime measure, an executive order. What the legal status of the newly emancipated slaves would be after the war was unclear, and the Proclamation had not freed the slaves in Delaware, Kentucky, Maryland, and Missouri, the four slave holding states that had not joined the Confederacy.

The impact of the abolition of slavery was massive. When the Thirteenth Amendment was ratified, all the slaves were suddenly free. Of course, as we all know that while the Thirteenth Amendment ended slavery, it didn't address racial discrimination. W.E.B. Du Bois wrote:

> Slavery was not abolished even after the Thirteenth Amendment. There were four million freedmen and most

of them on the same plantation, doing the same work they did before emancipation, except as their work had been interrupted and changed by the upheaval of war. Moreover, they were getting about the same wages and apparently were going to be subject to slave codes modified only in name. There were among them thousands of fugitives in the camps of the soldiers or on the streets of the cities, homeless, sick, and impoverished. They had been freed practically with no land nor money, and, save in exceptional cases, without legal status, and without protection

Look at the first sentence of the Thirteenth Amendment: "Neither slavery nor involuntary servitude except as a punishment for crime whereof the party shall have been duly convicted, shall exist within the United States, or any place subject to their jurisdiction." The Amendment permitted forced labor (chain gangs) as punishment for convicted criminals, and Southern states responded with "Black Codes." Codes, Douglas A. Blackmon, the author of *Slavery by Another Name*, called "an array of interlocking laws essentially intended to criminalize black life."

Southern states enacted all sorts of made-up laws intended to easily get black men in trouble so they could be arrested and forced to work for free. Especially popular were vagrancy laws, which allowed black men to be sentenced to forced labor for not having a job. For example, a Mississippi law required black workers to "contract with white farmers by January 1 of each year or face punishment for vagrancy." Laws as absurd as making it a crime for blacks to use obscene language or sell cotton after sunset were also enacted.

Life in the South could be brutally hard for the newly emancipated slaves. But there were a few notable success stories. Sara Breedlove, born in 1867, developed and marketed Madame C.J. Walker hair care products for black women. Breedlove, the daughter of two recently freed slaves became the United States' first self-made female millionaire. Madame C. J. Walker hair products, such as MADAM Revive and Reset Strengthening Shampoo and MCJW Madam CJ

Walker Hella Drenched Hydration Cream Co-Wash, can still be purchased today at stores like Walmart or from online retailers like Amazon.

The Thirteenth Amendment had opened the door for blacks, but the path to achieving the American Dream would be a hard road to follow. The Amendment started the American people on the road to the 1954 Supreme Court decision in *Brown v Board of Education of Topeka*, the passage of the 1964 Civil Rights Act and the 1965 Voting Rights Act. But the road to racial equality is one on which we are still walking.

The Thirteenth Amendment did more than free the slaves. It superseded Article 1, Section 2, Clause 3 of the Constitution under which each slave was counted as three-fifths of a person for the purpose of apportioning the number of House of Representative members for each state. Freed slaves were now counted the same as their white counterparts. As a result, for the purposes of Congressional representation, the population of the former Confederate States was substantially increased. This was a problem for the Republicans since southern whites voted for the Democrats. One possible solution was to try to get the newly freed slaves to vote Republican, but before this could happen the Republican controlled Congress needed to pass and send to the states for ratification, the Fourteenth Amendment.

The Fourteenth Amendment:
"I Have a Dream," the Fight for Civil Rights

The Fourteenth Amendment was ratified on July 9, 1868. It granted United States citizenship to all recently freed slaves, extended the due process provisions of the Fifth Amendment to the states and provided for equal protection under the law. It reads:

> All persons born or naturalized in the United States, and subject to the jurisdiction thereof, are citizens of the United States and of the state wherein they reside. No state shall make or enforce any law which shall abridge the privileges or immunities of citizens of the United States; nor shall any state deprive any person of life, liberty, or property, without due process of law; nor deny to any person within its jurisdiction the equal protection of the laws.
>
> Representatives shall be apportioned among the several states according to their respective numbers, counting the whole number of persons in each state, excluding Indians not taxed. But when the right to vote at any election for the choice of electors for President and Vice President of the United States, Representatives in Congress, the executive and judicial officers of a state, or the members of the legislature thereof, is denied to any of the male inhabitants of such state, being twenty-one years of age, and citizens of the United States, or in any way abridged, except for participation in rebellion, or other crime, the basis of representation therein shall be reduced in the proportion which the number of such male citizens shall bear to the whole number of male citizens twenty-one years of age in such state.
>
> No person shall be a Senator or Representative in Congress, or elector of President and Vice President, or hold any office, civil or military, under the United States, or under any state, who, having previously taken an oath, as a member of Congress, or as an officer of the United States, or as a member

of any state legislature, or as an executive or judicial officer of any state, to support the Constitution of the United States, shall have engaged in insurrection or rebellion against the same, or given aid or comfort to the enemies thereof. But Congress may by a vote of two-thirds of each House, remove such disability.

The validity of the public debt of the United States, authorized by law, including debts incurred for payment of pensions and bounties for services in suppressing insurrection or rebellion, shall not be questioned. But neither the United States nor any state shall assume or pay any debt or obligation incurred in aid of insurrection or rebellion against the United States, or any claim for the loss or emancipation of any slave; but all such debts, obligations and claims shall be held illegal and void.

The Congress shall have power to enforce, by appropriate legislation, the provisions of this article.

The first section of the Fourteenth Amendment includes the Citizenship, Privileges and Immunities, Due Process, and Equal Protection Clauses. The Citizenship Clause clarified the status of the recently freed slaves. They were citizens of the United States and the state in which they lived, the same as anyone else who had been born in the United States or had become a naturalized citizen of the United States.

Wong Kim Ark had been born on U.S. soil to Chinese parents. His parents were not American citizens. In 1894, Wong went to visit China but upon his return a year later, he was denied entry into the United States on the grounds that he was not an American citizen. Under the Chinese Exclusion Acts in effect at that time, citizens of China were prohibited from entering the United States. Wong was detained by order of the Port of San Francisco's Collector of Customs.

Wong insisted that he was a U.S. citizen, but he had to spend the next five months on a steam ship in port waiting to have his case heard. The District Court of the United States for the Northern District of California ruled that Wong was an American citizen, and it issued a writ of *habeas corpus* for Wong's release. The U.S. attorney appealed the decision to release Wong into the country, and the case went to the Supreme Court.

The question of the citizenship status of U.S.-born children of alien [non-citizen] parents had, up to this time, never been decided by the Supreme Court. The U.S. government argued that Wong's claim to U.S. citizenship "was of great importance, not just to Chinese Americans, but to all American citizens who had been born to alien parents." They were right, this case set a precedent for children born both to non-citizen residents who had entered the United States legally and to those who had entered the country illegally.

The Supreme Court, in *United States v Wong Kim Ark* (1898) considered the following question:

> Whether a child born in the United States, of parents of Chinese descent, who, at the time of his birth, are subjects of the Emperor of China, but have a permanent domicile and residence in the United States, and are there carrying on business, and are not employed in any diplomatic or official capacity under the Emperor of China, becomes at the time of his birth a citizen of the United States by virtue of the first clause of the Fourteenth Amendment of the Constitution,

In a 6–2 decision, the Court ruled that Wong was an American citizen. He successfully petitioned for his sons, born in China, to become American citizens. Wong's youngest son was drafted in the Second World War and later made a career in the U.S. Merchant Marines. Which again reminds us of all the potential benefits immigrants who become U.S. citizens bring to our society.

James C. Ho, a judge on the Fifth Circuit Court of Appeals, in a 2006 article, wrote:

> Birthright citizenship is guaranteed by the Fourteenth Amendment. That birthright is protected no less for children of undocumented persons than for descendants of *Mayflower* passengers.

There are those who oppose the idea that birthright citizenship should apply to the children of non-citizens. Some members of Congress from time to time propose legislation intended to deny citizenship at birth to U.S.-born children of foreign visitors, especially those who entered the country illegally.

One reason they object to birthright citizenship is birth tourism. The practice of traveling to another country for the purpose of having your baby there, so that your child will by birthright be a citizen of that country. As you can imagine, the U.S. is a popular destination. The Center for Immigration Studies estimates that there are over 30,000 babies born annually to women in the United States on tourist visas.

Being a U.S. citizen not only confers all the Constitutional rights, but also provides access to public schooling, healthcare, and perhaps most importantly sponsorship for the parents in the future. Children who are U.S. Citizens, once they turn eighteen, can petition to grant their parents permanent residence and eventual citizenship.

On January 20, 2025, his first day in office, President Donald Trump issued an executive order that restricted U.S. citizenship to only those children of non-citizen mothers who were legal permanent residents or whose fathers were United States citizens or lawful permanent residents. The implementation of Trump's order was immediately blocked by several Federal District Court judges on the grounds that it violates the Fourteenth Amendment's Citizenship Clause. Since the Justice Department will appeal, the Supreme Court will likely once again need to address the issue of birthright citizenship.

Privileges and Immunity Clause

The Privileges and Immunity Clause of the Fourteenth Amendment prevents States from making any laws that curtail in any way the "privileges and immunities of citizens of the United States." A state may not enact laws that abridge or abrogate the rights and protections guaranteed by the Constitution.

The Personal Responsibility and Work Opportunity Reconciliation Act of 1996 gave States, which received Temporary Assistance to Needy Families Funds, the option to pay the benefit amount of another State's program to residents who had lived in their State for less than one year. California announced it would start exercising this option, and Brenda Roe, who had been living in the State for less than one year, filed suit.

In *Saenz v Roe* (1999), the Supreme Court in a 7–2 decision ruled that California's attempt to enforce the Personal Responsibility and Work Opportunities Act's option to pay first-year residents different benefits than those paid to long-term residents violated the Fourteenth Amendment's Privileges and Immunities Clause. The Court ruled that

> The right to travel embraces three different components: the right to enter and leave another State; the right to be treated as a welcome visitor while temporarily present in another State; and, for those travelers who elect to become permanent residents, the right to be treated like other citizens of that State....
>
> The right of newly arrived citizens to the same privileges and immunities enjoyed by other citizens of their new State-the third aspect of the right to travel-is at issue here. That right is protected by the new arrival's status as both a state citizen and a United States citizen, and it is plainly identified in the Fourteenth Amendment's Privileges or Immunities Clause.

Justice John Paul Stevens who wrote the majority opinion for the Court pointed out that Justice Samuel Freeman Miller, in his majority opinion in the *Slaughter-House Cases* (1873), had explained that one of the privileges conferred by this Clause

> is that a citizen of the United States can, of his own volition, become a citizen of any State of the Union by a bona fide residence therein, with the same rights as other citizens of that State.

Due Process and Equal Protection Clauses

The Due Process and Equal Protection Clauses of the Fourteenth Amendment extend the due process and equal protections in the Bill of Rights to the states: "nor shall any state deprive any person of life, liberty, or property, without due process of law; nor deny to any person within its jurisdiction the equal protection of the laws."

Southern states chose to interpret the equal protection wording as a justification for segregation. The pretense was that while whites and blacks were kept separate, they were equal in all other respects. Nothing could have been further from the truth. Segregation in the south was inherently unequal.

In 1890, 22 years after the Fourteenth Amendment had been ratified, the state of Louisiana passed a Separate Car Act. The act required separate accommodations for blacks and whites traveling on railroads. Blacks couldn't sit in the same train car with whites. This sort of segregation was common in the post-Civil War south. Everything from making blacks sit in the back of buses, attend separate schools, use separate public restrooms, and even have to drink at separate public water fountains. Blacks were also not allowed to live in white neighborhoods, or eat at the same restaurants that whites ate at.

Homer Plessy described himself as "seven-eighths Caucasian and one-eighth African blood." In the late 1700s, his grandfather had emigrated to the United States from France, married a free black woman of color, and had eight children. One of his mixed-race grandchildren was Homer Plessy, a married shoemaker who on June 7, 1892, bought a first-class ticket from New Orleans to Covington and boarded a "Whites Only" car.

When the conductor asked Plessy for his ticket, he also asked Plessy if he was a colored man, and when Plessy said he was, he told Plessy to move to the Colored Peoples Car. Plessy refused. The conductor stopped the train, and Plessy was forcibly removed. This was a deliberate protest move and, like many protest moves, it got Plessy arrested and thrown in the Orleans Parish jail. He was found guilty and charged a fine of 25 dollars for violating the Separate Car Act.

But, as Plessy had probably hoped, his case eventually ended up in the Supreme Court. The question facing the Court was, did enforcing rules separating whites and blacks violate the Fourteenth Amendment's Equal Protection Clause?

In *Plessy v Ferguson* (1896), the Supreme Court, in arguably one of the worst, if not the worst decision ever handed down, ruled that segregation did not violate the Equal Protection Clause of the Fourteenth Amendment. Justice Henry Billings Brown delivered the 7–1 opinion:

> The object of the amendment was undoubtedly to enforce the absolute equality of the two races before the law, but, in the nature of things, it could not have been intended to abolish distinctions based upon color, or to enforce social, as distinguished from political, equality, or a commingling of the two races upon terms unsatisfactory to either. Laws permitting, and even requiring, their separation in places where they are liable to be brought into contact do not necessarily imply the inferiority of either race to the other, and have been generally, if not universally, recognized as within the competency of the state legislatures in the exercise of their police power. The most common instance of this is connected with the establishment of separate schools for white and colored children, which has been held to be a valid exercise of the legislative power even by courts of States where the political rights of the colored race have been longest and most earnestly enforced.

Justice John Marshall Harlan, the lone dissenting voice, called the Court's decision pernicious:

> Our Constitution is color-blind, and neither knows nor tolerates classes among citizens. In respect of civil rights, all citizens are equal before the law. The humblest is the peer of the most powerful. The law regards man as man, and takes no account of his surroundings or of his color when his civil rights

as guaranteed by the supreme law of the land are involved. It is therefore to be regretted that this high tribunal, the final expositor of the fundamental law of the land, has reached the conclusion that it is competent for a State to regulate the enjoyment by citizens of their civil rights solely upon the basis of race.

Homer Plessy was a shoemaker. He did not have a law degree. He was simply white enough to board the first-class car of a train, and black enough to be arrested for doing so. He unsuccessfully challenged state-sponsored racial segregation. With its decision in *Plessy*, the Supreme Court had legalized apartheid in the United States. It would be 1954, before the Court faced up to what a horrible mistake that decision had been. In 2022, the Governor of Louisiana posthumously pardoned Homer Plessy, and a historical marker now stands where he was arrested.

After *Plessy*, Separate but Equal became the mantra for the southern states. White and black children attended separate schools in seventeen states (Alabama, Arkansas, Delaware, Florida, Georgia, Kentucky, Louisiana, Maryland, Mississippi, Missouri, North Carolina, Oklahoma, South Carolina, Tennessee, Texas, Virginia, and West Virginia). Black children went to black schools, with their own facilities, budgets, and teachers, which in theory were equal to the schools that the white children attended, but in reality were anything but.

Enter Linda Brown, a black girl in the third grade living in Topeka Kansas. Elementary schools in Topeka were segregated, and Linda was attending Monroe Elementary School which, compared to most black schools, wasn't bad. But it was not as good as the white schools she wasn't allowed to attend. Which prompted Linda's father, Oliver Brown, to file suit against the Board of Education in Topeka, Kansas after his daughter was denied admission to a white elementary school.

The plaintiffs were thirteen angry parents, all of whom had attempted to enroll their children in the closest neighborhood elementary school in the fall of 1951. They were all refused and redirected to the segregated schools. Oliver Brown's daughter Linda had to walk six blocks to her school bus stop, and then ride the bus to her school because she was not allowed to attend the whites only elementary school that was only a few blocks from her home.

The lower courts relying on the decision in *Plessy* ruled against the plaintiffs. But in 1954, the Kansas case, along with other lawsuits challenging school segregation from Delaware, South Carolina, Virginia, and Washington, D.C. make it to the Supreme Court. The question before the Court in *Brown v Board of Education of Topeka* (1954) was, "Does segregation of children in public schools solely on the basis of race, even though the physical facilities and other 'tangible' factors may be equal, deprive the children of the minority group of equal educational opportunities?"

Thurgood Marshall, Chief Counsel of the National Association for the Advancement of Colored People (NAACP) Legal Defense and Education Fund, and later the first black appointed to the Supreme Court, argued the case for the plaintiffs. The Department of Justice filed a Friend of the Court (*amicus curiae*) brief in support of the plaintiffs on the grounds that segregation was hurting the image of the United States, that is, it was making us look bad to the rest of the world. Attorney General James P. McGranery wrote: "The existence of discrimination against minority groups in the United States has an adverse effect upon our relations with other countries. Racial discrimination furnishes grist for the Communist propaganda mills."

Remember, the 1950s was the height of the Cold War. The United States was in competition with the Soviets for the friendship and allegiance of countries that were gaining independence from colonial rule. Countries of non-white people. Justice William O. Douglas wrote that one of the things he had learned from his travels was that "the attitude of the United States toward its colored minorities is a powerful factor in our relations." Chief Justice Earl Warren, in a 1954 speech to the American Bar Association had said that "the extent to which we maintain the spirit of our constitution with its Bill of Rights, will in the long run do more to make it [the United States] both secure and the object of adulation than the number of hydrogen bombs we stockpile."

The Supreme Court struggled to reach consensus on *Brown*. Earl Warren, the Chief Justice, felt that the issue before the Court was so important that the Court needed to speak with one voice, and he worked tirelessly to get a unanimous ruling to reverse *Plessy*. He argued that the only reason to rule against the plaintiffs was if you believed in racial disparities—that is, whites were the superior race and blacks were the inferior one. He felt that only by ending segregation could the Court maintain its legitimacy, and only by ruling unanimously could it avoid a massive backlash from the South, and show the world that the United States is committed to equality. He got his way, and in *Brown*, the Court unanimously ruled that

> To separate [black children] from others of similar age and qualifications solely because of their race generates a feeling of inferiority as to their status in the community that may affect their hearts and minds in a way unlikely to ever be undone.
> ....
> We conclude that in the field of public education the doctrine of "separate but equal" has no place. Separate educational facilities are inherently unequal. Therefore, we hold that the plaintiffs and others similarly situated for whom the actions have been brought are, by reason of the segregation complained of, deprived of the equal protection of the laws guaranteed by the Fourteenth Amendment.

In 1955, the Court ordered desegregation to "proceed with all deliberate speed." But instead of compliance, there was massive resistance. In 1957, President Eisenhower ordered troops from the 101st Airborne Division to ensure the safety of nine black students who had enrolled in Little Rock, Arkansas' formerly all-white Central High School.

In *Griffin v County School Board of Prince Edward County* (1964), the Supreme Court ruled that Prince Edward County, Virginia's decision to close its public schools to avoid integrating them violated the Equal Protection Clause of the Fourteenth Amendment. And in *Plyler v Doe* (1982), the Court by a 5–4 decision ruled that a "Texas statute which withholds from local school districts any state funds for the education of children who were not "legally admitted" into the United States, and which authorizes local school districts to deny enrollment to such children, violates the Equal Protection Clause of the Fourteenth Amendment."

In his dissenting opinion, Chief Justice Warren Burger wrote: "Were it our business to set the Nation's social policy, I would agree without hesitation that it is senseless for an enlightened society to deprive any children—including illegal aliens—of an elementary education." But he argued the Constitution did not "vest in this Court the authority to strike down laws because they do not meet our standards of desirable social policy, "wisdom," or "common sense." He concluded: "The Court makes no attempt to disguise that it is acting to make up for Congress' lack of 'effective leadership' in dealing with the serious national problems caused by the influx of uncountable millions of illegal aliens across our borders."

In *Loving v Virginia* (1967), the Supreme Court addressed the question of whether Virginia's anti-miscegenation law that made interracial marriage a criminal offense violated the Equal Protection Clause of the Fourteenth Amendment. The Court unanimously ruled that it did. In the opinion for the Court Chief Justice Earl Warren wrote:

> There is patently no legitimate overriding purpose independent of invidious racial discrimination which justifies this classification. The fact that Virginia prohibits only interracial marriages involving white persons demonstrates that the racial classifications must stand on their own justification, as measures designed to maintain White Supremacy.... We have consistently denied the constitutionality of measures which restrict the rights of citizens on account of race. There can be no doubt that restricting the freedom to marry solely because

of racial classifications violates the central meaning of the Equal Protection Clause.

These statutes also deprive the Lovings of liberty without due process of law in violation of the Due Process Clause of the Fourteenth Amendment. The freedom to marry has long been recognized as one of the vital personal rights essential to the orderly pursuit of happiness by free men.

Warren concluded his opinion with the following:

> The Fourteenth Amendment requires that the freedom of choice to marry not be restricted by invidious racial discriminations. Under our Constitution, the freedom to marry, or not marry, a person of another race resides with the individual, and cannot be infringed by the State.

In *Reed v Reed* (1971), the Supreme Court unanimously ruled that an Idaho Probate Court's decision that "males must be preferred to females" in choosing administrators of estates "is to make the very kind of arbitrary legislative choice forbidden by the Equal Protection Clause of the Fourteenth Amendment."

In *Lawrence v Texas* (2003), the Supreme Court had ruled in a 6–3 decision that a Texas law that made homosexual conduct, even when private and consensual, a crime violated the Due Process Clause of the Fourteenth Amendment. In 2015, the Supreme Court was tasked with deciding if the Equal Protection and Due Process Clauses of the Fourteenth Amendment required a state both to license same-sex marriages, and also to recognize same-sex-marriages that were performed in another state. The Court in a 5–4 decision ruled that it did. Justice Anthony M. Kennedy delivered the opinion for the majority.

> No union is more profound than marriage, for it embodies the highest ideals of love, fidelity, devotion, sacrifice, and family. In forming a marital union, two people become something

greater than once they were. As some of the petitioners in these cases demonstrate, marriage embodies a love that may endure even past death. It would misunderstand these men and women to say they disrespect the idea of marriage. Their plea is that they do respect it, respect it so deeply that they seek to find its fulfillment for themselves. Their hope is not to be condemned to live in loneliness, excluded from one of civilization's oldest institutions. They ask for equal dignity in the eyes of the law. The Constitution grants them that right.

The Students for Fair Admissions, a nonprofit legal advocacy group, sued Harvard on the grounds that Harvard's race-based admissions program violated the Civil Rights Act of 1964 by discriminating against Asian Americans. In *Students for Fair Admissions v President and Fellows of Harvard College* (2023), the Supreme Court by a 6–3 majority ruled that Harvard's admissions program violated the Equal Protection Clause of the Fourteenth Amendment.

Chief Justice John Roberts in the opinion for the Court noted that Harvard's race-based admissions system fails "to comply with the twin commands of the Equal Protection Clause that race may never be used as a "negative and that it may not operate as a stereotype." In a separate concurring opinion, Justice Clarence Thomas wrote "that all forms of discrimination based on race—including so-called affirmative action—are prohibited under the Constitution."

The second section of the Fourteenth Amendment, the Apportionment of Representation Clause, states that if a State denies the right to vote to any male citizen, age 21 or older, for any reason other than being convicted of a crime or participating in a rebellion against the United States, then that State's population for the purposes of apportioning members of the House of Representatives will be reduced by the number of males denied the right to vote.

The third section, the Disqualification from Public Office Clause, bars any person from holding a Federal or State office if that person had previously sworn to defend the Constitution of the United States, but had subsequently engaged in an insurrection or rebellion or given aid and comfort to the enemies of the United States. However, by a two-thirds majority vote in the House and in the Senate, Congress may remove the restriction.

After the Civil War, in a spirit of reconciliation, a great many former Confederate officers and civilian officials were granted pardons. Two examples of post-Civil War reconciliation are especially worth mentioning. Fitzhugh Lee had served as a Confederate general, received a pardon, and was elected the 40th Governor of Virginia. During the Spanish American War, he was commissioned as a Major General of Volunteers. He commanded the 7th Army Corps, and oversaw the initial occupation of Cuba after the war. Lee retired as a brigadier general in the regular army.

Joseph Wheeler was also a Confederate general. After being pardoned he was elected to Congress and served as a member of the House from Alabama from 1881 to 1883 and from 1885 to 1899. When the Spanish-American War broke out, he was commissioned a major general of volunteers and commanded the U.S. cavalry in Cuba, was the senior member of the Commission that negotiated the surrender of the Spanish army in Cuba, and later commanded troops in the Philippines. Like Fitzhugh Lee, Wheeler retired as a brigadier general in the regular army.

Not everybody was pardoned, and some pardons came late. Robert E. Lee wasn't pardoned until 1975, 105 years after his death. Jefferson Davis who served as the Confederacy's president never received a pardon, but his statue stands in the U.S. Capitol's Statuary Hall, as does the statue of the Confederacy's vice president Alexander Hamilton Stephens. But one has to wonder for how much longer will the statues of men who tried to tear the country in half in order to preserve the vile institution of slavery be honored in the nation's Capital.

The Fourteenth Amendment's provision that bars anyone who has given aid or comfort to the enemies of the United States from holding federal office was used as the rationale to remove Victor Berger from his seat in Congress in November 1919. Berger was a founding member of the Socialist Party of America. In 1910, he was elected to the House of Representatives from Wisconsin's Fifth Congressional District. Berger lost his bid for reelection in 1912. An ardent anti-war critic, Berger was elected to the House again in 1918, even though he had been indicted in February 1918, eleven months after the United States had entered the First World War, for violating the Espionage Act. In 1919 after being found guilty, he was sentenced to 20 years in prison, and not allowed to take his seat in Congress.

Berger appealed his conviction. In *Berger v New York* (1921), the Supreme Court overturned Berger's conviction. The Court held that the judge who oversaw Berger's trial should have recused himself because of his personal bias against people of German descent. With his record now cleared, Berger again ran for Congress and was elected in 1922, and reelected in 1924 and 1926.

In December 2023, the Colorado Supreme Court concluded that Donald J. Trump had on his last day in office as President of the United States incited an insurrection against the United States, and that therefore in accordance with Section 3 of the Fourteenth Amendment, he was barred from holding a future federal office. The Colorado Supreme Court ordered the Colorado Secretary of State to not "list President Trump's name on the 2024 presidential primary ballot" or "count any write-in votes cast for him."

President Trump appealed and in *Trump v Anderson* (2024), the Supreme Court in a unanimous decision concluded that the "states have no power under the Constitution to enforce Section 3 with respect to federal offices, especially the presidency." That is, in accordance with Section 5 of the Fourteenth Amendment, only Congress has the power to enforce the provisions of Section 3 of the Amendment. In a concurring opinion, Justice Amy Coney Barrett wrote:

> In my judgment, this is not the time to amplify disagreement with stridency. The Court has settled a politically charged issue in the volatile season of a Presidential election. Particularly in this circumstance, writings on the Court should turn the

national temperature down, not up. For present purposes, our differences are far less important than our unanimity: All nine Justices agree on the outcome of this case. That is the message Americans should take home.

Section 4 of the Fourteenth Amendment, the Public Debt Clause, is a mouthful:

> The validity of the public debt of the United States, authorized by law, including debts incurred for payment of pensions and bounties for services in suppressing insurrection or rebellion, shall not be questioned. But neither the United States nor any State shall assume or pay any debt or obligation incurred in aid of insurrection or rebellion against the United States, or any claim for the loss or emancipation of any slave; but all such debts, obligations and claims shall be held illegal and void.

In 1860, the year before the Civil War started, the U.S. Government debt was around 65 million. But the Civil War was costly, and by April 1865 when it ended, the debt was 2.76 billion. Section 4 of the Fourteenth Amendment has been viewed as being more expansive than simply guaranteeing that the debt the U.S. Government ran up fighting the rebellion would be paid. The broader, and commonly accepted view, is that the United States will honor any future debt authorized by Congress.

Section 4 of the Fourteenth Amendment also prohibited payment of any debt incurred by the former Confederate States, and it also banned any payment to former slaveholders. Many slave owners wanted compensation for their losses. Interestingly enough, the United States, for a change, was not taking a page out of the English playbook. When Britain emancipated its slaves in 1839, the British empire compensated all the former slave owners to the tune of 30 million pounds. Some have wondered if the United States had done that in the 1850s would that have averted the Civil War.

Section 5 of the Fourteenth Amendment, the Enforcement Clause, gives Congress the "power to enforce, by appropriate legislation, the provisions" of Sections 1–4 of the Amendment. As previously mentioned, the Enforcement Clause was cited by the Supreme Court in deciding that States lack the power to use Section 3 of the Amendment as a rationale for denying candidates for federal office a place on the ballot.

In *City of Boerne v Flores* (1997), the Supreme Court limited the scope of the Religious Freedom Restoration Act, which Congress had enacted in 1993 to only federal action. The Court in a 6–3 decision held that while Section 5 of the Fourteenth Amendment gave Congress the power to remedy violations of rights enumerated in Sections 1–4 of the Amendment, it did not give Congress the power to create new rights or expand existing ones. Justice Anthony Kennedy in the opinion for the Court wrote:

> Congress' power under Section 5 extends only to enforcing the Fourteenth Amendment.
>
> Legislation which deters or remedies its constitutional violations can fall within the suite of Congress' enforcement power. However, Congress does not have the power to decree the substance of the Fourteenth Amendment's restrictions on the states. While the line between measures that remedy and prevent unconstitutional actions, and measures that make substantive change in the governing law is not easy to determine, and Congress must have a wide latitude in determining where it lies. The distinction exists and it must be observed. It must be congruent in proportionality between the injury to be prevented or remedied in the means adopted to that end. The Fourteenth Amendment's history and our case will confirm the remedial rather than substantive nature of the Enforcement Clause.

Kennedy then issued a not-so-subtle warning that acts of Congress that were counter to the Supreme Court's prior Constitutional rulings would not be well received.

> When Congress acts within its fair power and responsibility, it has not just the right but the duty to make its own informed judgment on the meaning and force of the Constitution. On the other hand, when the court has interpreted the Constitution, it has acted within the province of the Judicial Branch which embraces the duty to say what the law is. When the political branches of the government act against a background of a judicial interpretation of the constitutional already issued, it must be understood that in later cases and controversies, the court will treat its precedents with the respect due them under settled principles including *stare decisis* [to stand by things decided]. Contrary expectations must be disappointed.

In 1994, Congress enacted the Violence Against Women Act, which allowed women who had been victims of "gender-motivated violence" such as rape to file a civil suit against their attackers in federal court. In *United States v Morrison* (2000), the Supreme Court in a 5–4 decision ruled that Section 5 of the Fourteenth Amendment only gave Congress the power to regulate actions by States. In the opinion for the Court Chief Justice William Rehnquist wrote: "congress' enforcement power under Section 5 of the Fourteenth Amendment is limited to the regulation of states and state actors."

> Our cases have never departed from our original understanding of the Fourteenth Amendment state action requirement, because Section 13981 [of the Violence Against Women Act] regulates the conduct of private persons, not states or state officials; it cannot be sustained as an exercise with Congress' Section 5 authority.

The Enforcement Clause of the Fourteenth Amendment gave Congress the power to enact the Civil Rights Act of 1964, a sweeping piece of legislation that made segregation by businesses that cater to the public, e.g., restaurants and hotels, illegal. It banned segregation in public facilities, e.g., libraries and swimming pools. The Act also banned discrimination in employment based on race, religion, ethnicity, sex, age, or disability, and it created the Equal Employment Opportunity Commission (EEOC) to enforce the law.

The Fourteenth Amendment with its Citizenship, Due Process, Equal Protection, Privileges and Immunities, and Enforcement Clauses is an incredibly valuable addition to the rights guaranteed to all Americans by the Bill of Rights.

The Fifteenth Amendment: Voting Rights

The Fifteenth Amendment is succinct:

> The right of citizens of the United States to vote shall not be denied or abridged by the United States or by any State on account of race, color, or previous condition of servitude.
>
> The Congress shall have power to enforce this article by appropriate legislation.

Ratified on February 3, 1870, it gave black men the right to vote. And they did at least initially.

Thomas Mundy Peterson, who voted on March 31, 1870, in a Perth Amboy, New Jersey referendum on revising the city charter is believed to be the first black man to cast his vote following the Fifteenth Amendment's ratification. Years later, Peterson said that "one white man, upon seeing him vote, ripped up his own ballot and declared that the franchise was worthless if a Negro could do it."

In the years immediately following the end of the Civil War, the period known as Reconstruction, black men voted and they often voted for black men. Over 2,000 black men were elected to local, state, and federal offices. Sixteen served in Congress. But as Eric Foner, the DeWitt Clinton Professor Emeritus of History at Columbia University has pointed out, while the initial results of enfranchising blacks was "a remarkable accomplishment given that slavery was such a dominant institution before the Civil War... the history of the 15th Amendment also shows rights can never be taken for granted: Things can be achieved and things can be taken away."

On April 13, 1873, Easter Sunday, hundreds of white men attacked and killed an estimated 150 blacks in Colfax, Louisiana. The black men who were murdered that day were voters who had supported the newly elected governor of Louisiana. The murderers had supported his opponent.

White supremacists used violence and intimidation to prevent blacks from voting. That was an obvious tactic. But they also used more insidious tactics that had the appearance of legality. Beginning in 1890, southern states enacted Jim Crow laws that effectively disenfranchised black voters. Poll taxes that required citizens to pay a fee to register to vote were levied. Literacy tests were given to prospective voters. Grandfather clauses exempted whites who had been eligible to vote prior to 1866 and their lineal descendants from having to pay the poll tax or take the literacy test.

In *Guinn v United States* (1915), a unanimous Supreme Court ruled that Oklahoma's Voter Registration Act's grandfather clause "was repugnant to the Fifteenth Amendment and therefore null and void." Justice Edward White wrote that the grandfather clause "inherently brings discrimination based on race... since it is based purely on a period of time before the enactment of the Fifteenth Amendment and makes that period the controlling and dominant test of the right of suffrage."

In 1944, the Supreme Court addressed the question of whether a Texas law that allowed the Democratic party to restrict voting in Democratic Primary elections to white males was constitutional. In *Smith v Allwright*, the Court in an 8–1 decision ruled that white only primaries were unconstitutional. Justice Stanley Reed delivered the opinion for the Court:

> The United States is a constitutional democracy. Its organic law grants to all citizens a right to participate in the choice of elected officials without restriction by any state because of race. This grant to the people of the opportunity for choice is not to be nullified by a state through casting its electoral process in a form which permits a private organization to practice racial discrimination in the election. Constitutional rights would be of little value if they could be thus indirectly denied.

Literacy tests were designed to keep black men from voting because they were almost impossible to pass. For example, one question on the 1964 Louisiana Literacy Test was "Spell backwards, forwards." Another was "Print the word vote upside down, but in the correct order."

William W. Van Alstyne, a professor of law at Duke University, conducted an experiment in which he submitted four questions found on the Alabama voter's literacy test to "all professors currently teaching constitutional law in American law schools." He asked that respondents take the test without using any references; just as a prospective voter would. He received 96 responses, and only 21 of those would have passed the test.

The sad reality is, although unfair, the use of literacy tests prevented black Americans from voting. In 1965, Congress using the power granted to it by Section 2, the Enforcement Clause of the Fifteenth Amendment passed the Voting Rights Act. The Act prohibits state and local governments from taking any action that "results in the denial or abridgement of the right of any citizen to vote on account of race or color." The Voting Rights Act specifically bans the use of literacy tests.

The voting Rights Act contains a preclearance provision, that is, before states and local jurisdictions with a history of racial discrimination can make any changes to their voting laws, they must first receive approval of those proposed changes from the U.S. Department of Justice. In *South Carolina v Katzenbach* (1966), the Supreme Court upheld the constitutionality of the preclearance provision, but in *Shelby County v Holder* (2013), the Court in a 5–4 decision struck down the preclearance provision. Chief Justice John Roberts in the opinion for the Court began by calling the Voting Rights Act "a resounding success."

> You will recall the 7% registration figure for African-Americans in Mississippi in 1965, it was 76% in 2004. As for the gap of 63 percentage points between African-American and white voter registration in that state in 1965, there was a gap in 2004 of about 4%, but it was in favor of African-American registration. There are examples of progress, more poignant than the numbers. During the freedom summer of 1964 in Philadelphia, Mississippi, three men were murdered while working in the area to register African-American

voters. On bloody Sunday in Selma, Alabama in 1965, police beat and used tear gas on hundreds marching in support of enfranchising African-Americans. Today, both Philadelphia, Mississippi and Selma, Alabama have African-Americans mayors. No one doubts that there is still voting discrimination in the South and in the rest of the country. As noted when we upheld the original Act, we said that exception conditions can justify legislative measures not otherwise appropriate. The question is whether the extraordinary measures of preclearance and desperate treatment of the states that were upheld 45 years ago remained constitutional in light of today's changed conditions.

Roberts concluded that they did not.

The Fifteenth Amendment commands that the right to vote shall not be denied or abridged on account of race or color, and it gives Congress the power to enforce that command. The Amendment is not designed to punish for the past; its purpose is to ensure a better future.

....

Regardless of how to look at the record no one can fairly say that it shows anything approaching the 'pervasive', 'flagrant', 'widespread', and 'rampant' discrimination that faced Congress in 1965, and that clearly distinguished the covered jurisdictions from the rest of the nation.

Justice Ruth Bader Ginsberg disagreed with the Courts decision that the preclearance requirement was no longer constitutional, and that Section 2 of the Fifteenth Amendment did not give Congress the authority to enforce it. In her dissenting opinion, she wrote: "Throwing out preclearance when it has worked and is continuing to work to stop discriminatory changes is like throwing away your umbrella in a rainstorm because you are not getting wet."

The Fifteenth Amendment was another major step toward ensuring equal treatment for all Americans. Grandfather clauses, white only primaries, and literacy tests were history. But the poll tax still had to be addressed.

The Twenty-Fourth Amendment: Eliminating the Poll Tax

Ratified on January 23, 1964, the Twenty Fourth Amendment abolished the poll tax. It reads:

> The right of citizens of the United States to vote in any primary or other election for President or Vice President, for electors for President or Vice President, or for Senator or Representative in Congress, shall not be denied or abridged by the United States or any State by reason of failure to pay poll tax or other tax.
>
> The Congress shall have power to enforce this article by appropriate legislation.

The legality of the poll tax had been upheld by the Supreme Court's decision in the 1937 case, *Breedlove v Suttles*. The Court in a unanimous decision held that "the payment of poll taxes as a prerequisite to voting is a familiar and reasonable regulation long enforced in many states." Justice Pierce Butler, in the opinion for the Court, wrote:

> To make payment of poll taxes a prerequisite of voting is not to deny any privilege or immunity protected by the Fourteenth Amendment. Privilege of voting is not derived from the United States, but is conferred by the state and, save as restrained by the Fifteenth and Nineteenth Amendments and other provisions of the Federal Constitution, the state may condition suffrage as it deems appropriate.

The Twenty-Fourth Amendment superseded the decision in *Breedlove* and outlawed the imposition of a poll tax in federal elections. The scope of the Amendment was then extended when, in *Harper v Virginia State Board of Elections* (1966), the Court in a 6-3 decision ruled that the imposition of a poll tax or any other tax in not just federal, but also in state and local elections violated the Equal Protection Clause of the Fourteenth Amendment. Justice William O. Douglas delivered the opinion for the Court:

> We conclude that a State violates the Equal Protection Clause of the Fourteenth Amendment whenever it makes the affluence of the voter or payment of any fee an electoral standard. Voter qualifications have no relation to wealth nor to paying or not paying this or any other tax. Our cases demonstrate that the Equal Protection Clause of the Fourteenth Amendment restrains the States from fixing voter qualifications which invidiously discriminate.
>
> ....
>
> We say the same whether the citizen, otherwise qualified to vote, has $1.50 in his pocket or nothing at all, pays the fee or fails to pay it. The principle that denies the State the right to dilute a citizen's vote on account of his economic status or other such factors, by analogy, bars a system which excludes those unable to pay a fee to vote or who fail to pay.

The Ronald Reagan Presidential Library and Museum website summed up its discussion of the Twenty-Fourth Amendment with the following:

> The Twenty-Fourth Amendment was one additional step in the pursuit of civil rights in the turbulent 1960s. Coincidentally, the new amendment was passed the same year as the Civil Rights Act, which outlawed all forms of discrimination across the United States, effectively ending the Segregation-era. Just one year after the new amendment's ratification, the Voting Rights Act of 1965 eliminated all forms of discrimination in voting for all American men and women, making voting a Constitutional right with no reservations for the first time in American history. The Twenty-fourth Amendment was instrumental in advancing the pursuit of voting rights, not

just for the political movements that preceded it, but also as a foundation for those that would follow.

The Thirteenth, Fourteenth, Fifteenth, and Twenty-Fourth Amendments were all steps on the road to equal rights for all Americans. A road on which, as previously noted, we are still walking.

CHAPTER 8

MONEY MAKES THE WORLD GO ROUND: THE SIXTEENTH, SEVENTEENTH, AND TWENTY-SEVENTH AMENDMENTS

These amendments gave Congress the power to levy a tax on income, changed the method by which United States Senators were elected, and set conditions for raising the salaries of members of Congress.

The Sixteenth Amendment:
Paying Uncle Sam, Income Taxes

The Constitution was adopted on June 21, 1788. In a letter to his friend, Jean Baptiste le Roy, written in November 1789, Benjamin Franklin expressed cautious optimism about the fate of the new republic:

> Our new Constitution is now established, everything seems to promise it will be durable; but, in this world, nothing is certain except death and taxes.

Article I of the Constitution (the Taxing Clause) gives Congress the "Power to lay and collect Taxes, Duties, Imposts and Excises... but all Duties, Imposts and Excises shall be uniform throughout the United States." While Congress had the power to levy taxes, Article I states that direct taxes, that is, taxes on income or property, "shall be apportioned among the several States ...according to their respective Numbers."

Prior to the ratification of the Sixteenth Amendment the Federal Government derived almost all of its revenue from tariffs and excise taxes. In 1894, Congress passed a Revenue Act (the Wilson–Gorman Tariff) that included a provision that allowed the Federal Government to levy a 2% tax on individuals with annual incomes of over $4,000. The tax was challenged in the courts.

In n *Pollock v Farmers' Loan and Trust Company* (1895), the Supreme Court in a 5–4 decision ruled that the income tax provision of the Revenue Act was unconstitutional because it violated the conditions set forth in Article I of the Constitution that direct taxes "be apportioned among the several states." Chief Justice Melville Weston Fuller delivered the opinion for the Court:

> It is not doubted that property owners ought to contribute in just measure to the expenses of the government. As to the States and their municipalities, this is reached largely through the imposition of direct taxes. As to the Federal government, it is attained in part through excises and indirect taxes upon luxuries and consumption generally, to which direct taxation may be added to the extent the rule of apportionment allows.

Justice John Marshall Harlan in his dissent noted that the Court's decision made the need for a constitutional amendment a necessity:

> When, therefore, this court adjudges, as it does now adjudge, that congress cannot impose a duty or tax upon personal property, or upon income arising either from rents of real estate or from personal property, including invested personal property, bonds, stocks, and investments of all kinds, except by apportioning the sum to be so raised among the states according to population, it practically decides that, without an amendment of the constitution,—two-thirds of both houses of congress and three-fourths of the states concurring,—such

property and incomes can never be made to contribute to the support of the national government.

Congress took 14 years to get around to writing the amendment to the Constitution that, as Justice Harlan had noted, the Court's decision in *Pollock* required in order for Congress to levy taxes without being bound to "the rule of apportionment." On July 2, 1909, Congress passed and sent to the states the Sixteenth Amendment.

The Sixteenth Amendment gave Congress the power to levy an income tax without apportioning the revenue among the states and without needing to take population into account. It was ratified on February 3, 1913. It reads:

> The Congress shall have power to lay and collect taxes on incomes, from whatever source derived, without apportionment among the several States, and without regard to any census or enumeration.

After the Amendment was ratified, Congress passed the Revenue Act of 1913 which levied a progressive federal income tax. The Act was challenged, and in *Brushaber v Union Pacific Railroad Co.* (1916), a unanimous Supreme Court ruled that the Sixteenth Amendment gave Congress the power to levy taxes on incomes without apportioning them among the states. In his opinion upholding the Revenue Act, Chief Justice Edward D. White wrote: "there can be no dispute that there was power by virtue of the Amendment during that period to levy the tax, without apportionment."

Since the ratification of the Sixteenth Amendment, the individual income tax has become the federal government's largest source of revenue. For fiscal year 2022, fifty-four percent of the money collected by the federal government were from individuals. Corporate income taxes accounted for another nine percent and payroll taxes (Social Security and Medicare) made up another thirty percent. The remainder came from consumption (tariffs and excise) taxes (two percent) and other revenue, such as property taxes and national park entrance fees (five percent).

In fiscal year 2024, the federal government took in $2.19 trillion in revenue, and it spent $3.25 trillion. The $1.06 trillion deficit was added to the national debt which in March 2024 stood at $34.59 trillion. As of February 28, 2025, it had grown to $36.22 trillion. Congress regularly has heated debates about raising or lowering personal and corporate income taxes, and over whether or not to raise the debt ceiling, but in the end, it always does raise it. Some have questioned whether a debt ceiling is necessary or even if it is constitutional. They point to the first sentence of Section 4 of the Fourteenth Amendment: "The validity of the public debt of the United States, authorized by law, including debts incurred for payment of pensions and bounties for services in suppressing insurrection or rebellion, shall not be questioned." And make the argument that the Fourteenth Amendment obligates the United States to pay its debts however large they may be, so an artificial debt ceiling is superfluous.

The ratification of the Sixteenth Amendment paved the way for Congress to authorize the Treasury Department to collect huge sums of money. Derek Bok, the former President of Harvard University, observed that the one thing that compulsive gamblers and universities have in common is that they never have enough money. The same can be said for governments.

The Seventeenth Amendment: The People Choose Their Senators

The Seventeenth Amendment provides for the direct election of United States Senators. Ratified on April 8, 1913, it reads:

> The Senate of the United States shall be composed of two Senators from each State, elected by the people thereof, for six years; and each Senator shall have one vote. The electors in each State shall have the qualifications requisite for electors of the most numerous branch of the State legislatures.
>
> When vacancies happen in the representation of any State in the Senate, the executive authority of such State shall issue writs of election to fill such vacancies: *Provided*, That the legislature of any State may empower the executive thereof to make temporary appointments until the people fill the vacancies by election as the legislature may direct.
>
> This amendment shall not be so construed as to affect the election or term of any Senator chosen before it becomes valid as part of the Constitution.

Prior to the ratification of the Seventeenth Amendment, in accordance with Article I, Section 3 of the Constitution, senators were chosen by state legislatures. The Framers were concerned about having a federal government that ran roughshod over the states. George Mason felt that having senators elected by their state legislatures would prevent the federal government from intrusions into the internal affairs of state governments.

When you think of the men elected by their legislatures in the early days of the republic, Henry Clay, John C. Calhoun, and Daniel Webster are names that immediately come to mind. There were other distinguished senators like Stephen Douglas, a Democrat, who in the fall of 1858 had seven debates, each in a different city, with his Republican opponent, Abraham Lincoln, to determine whether the Democrats or Republicans would control the Illinois state legislature.

In the election of 1858, the Democrats retained control of the Illinois General Assembly and Douglas was reelected to the Senate by a vote of 54–46.

The election of senators by state legislatures had its downsides. Sometimes there was legislative gridlock, and there was corruption. Men who would buy Senate seats. They would bribe legislators to vote for them so they could go to Washington and have all the perks of being a corrupt politician.

Men like William Lorimer, a Republican. He was elected to the Senate by the Illinois House of Representatives in March 1909. A 1910 *Chicago Tribune* article claimed that he had given a Democratic State Legislator $1,000 to vote for him in that election. Two Senate investigations and a few heated debates on the Senate floor later, the U.S. Senate adopted a resolution declaring "that corrupt methods and practices were employed in his election, and that election therefore, was invalid." Lorimer was expelled from office on July 13, 1912, just two months after Congress had passed the Seventeenth Amendment and sent it to the states for ratification.

Public disgust with corrupt politicians, exemplified by the Lorimer case, coupled with the social activism of the early twentieth-century progressive movement, led to the ratification of the Seventeenth Amendment in just eleven months. Having United States Senators elected directly by the voters was a major step in the right direction. But while state legislators are no longer being bribed by politicians seeking senate seats, having senators elected by the people doesn't prevent the occasional bad apple from getting into office.

Democrat Senator from Maryland Daniel Brewster served in the Senate from 1963 to 1969. In 1969, he was indicted by the U.S. Department of Justice on ten criminal counts of solicitation and acceptance of bribes. The Federal District Court judge granted Brewster's motion to dismiss the charges on the grounds that the Constitution's Speech or Debate Clause protected him "from any prosecution for alleged bribery to perform a legislative act."

The Department of Justice appealed, and in *United States v Brewster* (1972), the Supreme Court reversed the District Court's decision. Chief Justice Warren E. Burger wrote: "Taking a bribe is, obviously, no part of the legislative process or function; it is not a legislative act. It is not, by any conceivable interpretation, an act performed as a part of or even incidental to the role of a legislator."

In 1975, Brewster pleaded no contest to a single misdemeanor charge of accepting an illegal gratuity "without corrupt intent." So, is it possible to accept an illegal gratuity with any other intent? Brewster was fined and allowed to keep his law license.

David Durenberger was a Republican Senator from Minnesota from 1978 to 1995. He was indicted for misuse of public funds. He received reimbursement of $40,000 from the Senate for staying at a condo that he owned where he liked to go fishing. He also received ridiculous amounts of money for speaking engagements, over $100,000 for showing up and giving a speech. In 1990, the Senate voted 96–0 to censure him. In 1995, he pled guilty to five misdemeanors related to the misuse of public funds while he was a senator and was fined $1,000 and sentenced to a year of probation. Not much of a punishment for stealing taxpayer money. And if the news back then was any indication, many Americans wondered how many of his colleagues that voted to denounce him were getting away with similar illegal perks.

Bob Menendez was first elected to the Senate from New Jersey in 2006. He was indicted on federal corruption charges for failing to disclose gifts from an ophthalmologist, Dr. Salomon Meglan, on whose behalf he had done political favors. His trial in September 2017, ended in a mistrial when the jury could not reach a unanimous verdict. But don't worry, he didn't completely escape justice. The U.S. Senate Select Committee on Ethics wrote him a sternly worded letter. In that letter, the Committee stated the following:

> The Committee has found that over a six-year period you knowingly and repeatedly accepted gifts of significant value from Dr. Melgen without obtaining required Committee approval and that you failed to publicly disclose certain gifts as required by Senate Rule and federal law. Additionally, while

accepting these gifts, you used your position as a Member of the Senate to advance Dr. Melgen's personal and business interests. The Committee has determined that this conduct violated Senate Rules, federal law, and applicable standards of conduct. Accordingly, the Committee issues you this Public Letter of Admonition and also directs you to repay the fair market value of all impermissible gifts not already repaid.

In 2023, while still serving in the Senate, Menendez was indicted again. This time by the U.S. Attorney for the Southern District of New York:

> Robert Menendez Allegedly Agreed to Use His Official Position to Benefit Wael Hana, Jose Uribe, Fred Daibes, and the Government of Egypt in Exchange for Hundreds of Thousands of Dollars of Bribes to Menendez and His Wife Nadine Menendez, Which Included Gold Bars, Cash, and a Luxury Convertible.

On July 16, 2024, following a nine-week trial, Menendez was convicted of bribery, foreign agent, and obstruction of justice offences, and sentenced to eleven years in prison. Following his conviction, he resigned from the Senate. Justice delayed is still justice served.

The occasional bad apple aside, the men and women who serve in the United States Senate as do their counterparts in the House of Representatives do just that. They serve. They serve the people who elected them, and thanks to the Seventeenth Amendment, U.S. Senators are elected by and accountable to the people.

The Twenty-Seventh Amendment:
Not So Fast, Congressional Salaries

The most recent amendment to the Constitution, the Twenty-Seventh, was one of the original twelve amendments written by James Madison, passed by Congress, and sent to the states for ratification on September 25, 1789. It was ratified over 202 years later on May 7, 1992. It reads:

> No law, varying the compensation for the services of the Senators and Representatives, shall take effect, until an election of representatives shall have intervened.

Any increase in pay for legislators must take place after an election. Why do we have this amendment? Because members of Congress decide what their salary should be. The Twenty-Seventh Amendment does not stop members of Congress from voting themselves a pay raise, but it does keep them from getting it until after the next election. Which means if constituents are unhappy that their representatives have voted to raise their salaries, they can vote them out of office.

The Amendment languished until in 1982, Gregory Watson, a 19-year-old sophomore at the University of Texas, Austin, wrote a paper in which he argued that the Amendment Madison had proposed so long ago was still "live" and could be ratified. He got a C. But his paper wasn't graded by the teacher, it was graded by the teacher's assistant. Watson appealed the grade to the course instructor, but she agreed with the teaching assistant and let the C stand. Perhaps in anger, Watson started a letter-writing campaign to State Legislatures asking them to ratify Madison's Amendment.

Watson used what he had written in his paper as ammunition. This included the 1939 Supreme Court case, *Coleman v Miller*. In that case, the Court had ruled that questions regarding amendments to the Constitution "should be regarded as a political question pertaining to the political departments, with the ultimate authority in the Congress in the exercise of its control over the promulgation of the amendment." In other words, it was up to Congress, not the courts, to determine if an amendment with no time limit for ratification was still viable.

When Watson began his campaign in early 1982, he was aware of ratification by only six states. But he quickly discovered that it had been ratified by a few more states. Wyoming had ratified the Amendment in 1978, as a protest against a 1977 Congressional pay raise. Kentucky, on the other hand, had ratified the amendment in 1792, something Kentucky lawmakers must have forgotten about because the Kentucky General Assembly ratified the Amendment again in 1996.

Most of the responses Watson initially received were negative. State Legislators believed the Amendment was too old, or that no one would get behind it. More often than not, he just never got a reply. Then Senator William Cohen responded. He passed the Amendment on to someone back home, who passed it on to someone else, who then introduced it in the Maine Legislature. And in 1983, state lawmakers ratified it. Watson worked tirelessly for ten years, and wrote a lot of letters. In May 1992, his efforts paid off when Michigan became the thirty-eighth state to ratify the Twenty-Seventh Amendment.

Twenty-five years later, in 2017, the University of Texas changed the grade on Watson's paper to an A. Not all heroes wear capes.

The Twenty-Seventh Amendment, written by James Madison in 1789, prevents members of Congress from arbitrarily voting themselves pay raises without their constituents being able to register their approval or disapproval. Members of Congress cannot receive any salary increase they vote to give themselves unless they are reelected.

CHAPTER 9

TO DRINK OR NOT TO DRINK, THAT IS THE QUESTION: THE EIGHTEENTH AND TWENTY-FIRST AMENDMENTS

The Eighteenth Amendment banned the sale and distribution of alcoholic beverages. The Twenty-First Amendment repealed the Eighteenth Amendment.

The Eighteenth Amendment: Banning Booze

The Eighteenth Amendment was passed by Congress and sent to the States on December 18, 1917. It was ratified on January 16, 1919. It reads:

> After one year from the ratification of this article the manufacture, sale, or transportation of intoxicating liquors within, the importation thereof into, or the exportation thereof from the United States and all territory subject to the jurisdiction thereof for beverage purposes is hereby prohibited.
> The Congress and the several States shall have concurrent power to enforce this article by appropriate legislation.
> This article shall be inoperative unless it shall have been ratified as an amendment to the Constitution by the legislatures of the several States, as provided in the Constitution, within

seven years from the date of the submission hereof to the States by the Congress.

In other words, no more booze. You can't buy it, you can't sell it, you can't bring it in or out of the country, and you certainly can't drink it. Thus begins Prohibition, often referred to as "The Noble Experiment." Why outlaw alcohol for everyone in the United States? To reduce crime and corruption. After all, drunk people make bad decisions. To solve social problems. Drunk people lose their jobs or don't take care of their families.

In the early Twentieth Century, the Woman's Christian Temperance Union and the Catholic Total Abstinence Union of America wanted to turn everyday into Sunday, a day of temperance and virtue. They were assisted in their efforts to outlaw the manufacture and sale of alcoholic beverages by the Anti-Saloon League, which under the direction of its president Wayne Wheeler, conducted one of, if not the most, effective lobbying campaign in American history.

The League lobbied members of Congress and state legislators. It supported "dry" candidates and did its best to defeat "wet" ones. In a time before, radio, television, and the Internet, it used the press, posters, and pamphlets to sway public opinion. It even used the United States' involvement in the First World War to somehow convince legislators and the general public that outlawing liquor was the patriotic thing to do. Largely because of its efforts, Congress passed the Eighteenth Amendment on December 18, 1917, and sent it to the states for ratification.

In fairness, anecdotal evidence indicates that Americans drank more back then. Regardless, alcohol had been a contentious topic in America since way before the Eighteenth Amendment. In 1791, Congress had passed the "Whiskey Tax," a tax on what was then America's most popular beverage.

Why was whiskey more popular than, say, beer? Because it didn't spoil and was easier to make. Farmers who had a surplus of almost any grain, rye, barley, wheat, or corn could ferment it and make whiskey.

The Whiskey Tax was levied only a few years after the revolution. The United States was in debt for the money we had borrowed to support the war effort to defeat Britain. The Whiskey Tax was intended to generate revenue to help take care of that debt. But there was another group who got behind this legislation. A group that didn't care about the fact that the United States had debts totaling $54,000,000. They were deeply religious people and social reformers who hoped that a "sin tax" would get people to stop drinking that "Devil Juice."

Naturally, whiskey distillers objected to the tax. In fact, many refused to pay it, and when agents of the federal government tried to collect the tax, they ended up being beaten, and even tarred and feathered. The Whiskey Rebellion was centered in Western Pennsylvania. It was put down quickly without a shot being fired by the arrival of a large body of federal troops under the command of Major General Daniel Morgan, a Revolutionary War hero, and the victor at the 1781 Battle of Cowpens.

Two of the leaders of the rebellion were convicted of treason and sentenced to be hanged, but they were pardoned by President Washington. He better than most understood why Americans would fight against what they perceived to be an unfair tax. Thomas Jefferson had been opposed to the imposition of an excise tax on whiskey. In a letter to James Madison, he sounded almost sympathetic to the rebels: "I hold it that a little rebellion now and then is a good thing, and as necessary in the political world as storms in the physical. It is a medicine necessary for the sound health of government." In 1802, Congress repealed the Whiskey Tax.

By the time, the Eighteenth Amendment was ratified, Americans were used to paying liquor taxes. The Federal Government derived from thirty to forty percent of its revenue from them, and for many states, the percentage of tax revenue generated by taxes on liquor was even higher. But for the ratification of the Sixteenth Amendment which allowed the feds and the states to offset the loss of revenue from liquor taxes by levying income taxes, it is highly unlikely that the Eighteenth Amendment would have been ratified.

Prohibition was all about getting rid of a social vice. Ironically, this rush to eliminate alcohol and all the ills caused by its consumption created a whole new set of problems. The Eighteenth Amendment specified that one year after the date it was ratified, no alcoholic beverages (intoxicating liquors) could be imported, exported, manufactured, distributed, or sold in the United States. Which meant one thing, time to stock up!

People had one year to get rid of their liquor, or to buy and stock up their secret supply before the Amendment went into effect. After that, all bets were off. Almost overnight speakeasies—illegal bars—were popping up all over America. Moonshine, alcohol made in home stills, became a cottage industry. Sadly, some of it caused blindness and paralysis. There were an estimated 1,000 deaths a year from drinking bathtub gin.

The Eighteenth Amendment forced the nation's breweries, distilleries, and saloons to go out of business, and as a result, thousands of people lost their jobs. The entertainment industry has glamorized the Roaring Twenties, but Prohibition was the start of an economic disaster for many legitimate business owners and their employees. However, it also made some people a lot of money.

Men like Al Capone, which brings us to another problem created by Prohibition: organized crime. Capone ran a syndicate in Chicago during the 1920s and made a fortune controlling the sale of illegal booze. He is estimated to have made $100 million a year during prohibition.

Interestingly enough, the term "organized crime" didn't really exist in the United States before prohibition. The criminal gangs that existed prior to prohibition were generally involved in extortion, gambling, and prostitution. Often, they took their orders from the politicians who ran the big cities. In exchange for local law enforcement looking the other way, gang members beat up political rivals and intimidated voters.

Prohibition changed all that. Bootlegging and control of the acquisition, distribution, and sale of liquor were big businesses. The gangs that ran them needed the ability to operate across state and international borders. Huge sums of money needed to be laundered, and bribes needed to be paid. It is estimated that during the heyday of the Prohibition Era, Al Capone was spending $500,000 a month in bribes, and that was in addition to the booze and the prostitutes that were part of the total package. And once the dirty cop or crooked politician was in your pocket, the threat of blackmail was sure to keep him there.

Gangs also engaged in turf wars. Sometimes these were resolved peacefully, but sometimes they ended in deadly violence. Capone is believed to have ordered the St. Valentine's Day massacre in which seven members of Chicago's North Side Gang were shot dead. Capone was arrested in 1931 and tried, not for murder or racketeering, but for tax evasion. He was sentenced to eleven years in prison and was released after serving eight. Debilitated by syphilis, he had a stroke followed by a heart attack and died in 1947. Visitors to Alcatraz can see Capone's cell.

Prohibition cost the Federal Government an estimated $11 billion in lost liquor tax revenues. You can't tax something people aren't allowed to buy. You can confiscate it, but then you have to throw it away. Federal, state, and local governments turned to the income tax to make up the shortfall. Moreover, instead of achieving the intended result, abstinence, alcohol consumption actually increased.

Winston Churchill called Prohibition "an affront to the whole history of mankind." And H.L. Mencken summed up the effect the Eighteenth Amendment had on the nation this way:

> There is not less drunkenness in the Republic, but more. There is not less crime, but more. There is not less insanity, but more. The cost of government is not smaller, but vastly greater. Respect for law has not increased, but diminished.

The American people, Congress, and the State Legislatures had finally had enough. Fed up with the "Noble Experiment," they ended Prohibition. Organized criminal gangs, no longer able to make their illegal proceeds from the distribution and sale of alcohol, didn't go away. They simply entered other businesses, like drug and sex trafficking.

The Twenty-First Amendment:
You Can Have a Drink Again

The Twenty-First Amendment was ratified on December 5, 1933. In his campaign for the presidency in 1932, Franklin Delano Roosevelt had said that it was "time to correct the 'stupendous blunder'" that was Prohibition." The Twenty-First Amendment did that. It reads:

> The eighteenth article of amendment to the Constitution of the United States is hereby repealed.
>
> The transportation or importation into any State, Territory, or Possession of the United States for delivery or use therein of intoxicating liquors, in violation of the laws thereof, is hereby prohibited.
>
> This article shall be inoperative unless it shall have been ratified as an amendment to the Constitution by conventions in the several States, as provided in the Constitution, within seven years from the date of the submission hereof to the States by the Congress.

Upon hearing that the Amendment had been ratified, FDR is reputed to have said, "What America needs now is a drink."

Section 2 of the Twenty-First Amendment has been interpreted by the courts as allowing states and local jurisdictions to set their own rules regarding the sale of alcoholic beverages. There are seventeen states that exercise some or total control over the sale of alcoholic beverages, usually through state-run or state-licensed Alcohol Beverage Control (ABC) stores. There are still over eighty dry counties, that is, where the sale of alcoholic beverages is prohibited.

Prohibition was ended, but a new sport rose from its ashes, stock car racing. Bootleggers during Prohibition needed cars that could outrun the police. They would modify ordinary-looking sedans by installing V-8 engines, stripping out the seats so as to make room for more cases of liquor and adding extra suspension coils to handle the added weight. Then all they had to do was put the peddle to the metal on back roads where there were fewer police patrolling than on the main highways.

Bootleggers needed to be excellent drivers since they were often required to speed along curved mountain roads and dirt paths, often at night with their lights off to avoid being spotted. Even before Prohibition came to an end in 1933, the drivers had started having races, usually on weekends on dirt tracks. And these races started attracting an audience. Those races eventually evolved into the National Association for Stock Car Auto Racing. NASCAR, established in 1947, was an unpredictable result of the Eighteenth Amendment.

Historian Michael Lerner summed up the lessons to be learned from Prohibition in these words:

> There is little doubt that Prohibition failed to achieve what it set out to do, and that its unintended consequences were far more far reaching than its few benefits. The ultimate lesson is two-fold. Watch out for solutions that end up worse than the problems they set out to solve, and remember that the Constitution is no place for experiments, noble or otherwise.

CHAPTER 10

NEW VOTERS: THE NINETEENTH, TWENTY-THIRD, AND TWENTY-SIXTH AMENDMENTS

These amendments extended voting rights to women and eighteen-year-olds, and gave residents of the District of Columbia the right to vote in presidential elections.

The Nineteenth Amendment: Women's Suffrage

The Nineteenth Amendment was ratified on August 18, 1920. It reads:

> The right of citizens of the United States to vote shall not be denied or abridged by the United States or by any State on account of sex.
>
> Congress shall have power to enforce this article by appropriate legislation.

Elizabeth Cady Stanton organized the first women's rights convention in the United States. Held in Seneca Falls, New York on July 19 and 20, 1848, it ended with the attendees signing a Declaration of Sentiments which included the following:

> The history of mankind is a history of repeated injuries and usurpations on the part of man toward woman, having in

direct object the establishment of an absolute tyranny over her. To prove this, let facts be submitted to a candid world.

He has never permitted her to exercise her inalienable right to the elective franchise.

He has compelled her to submit to laws, in the formation of which she had no voice.

He has withheld from her rights which are given to the most ignorant and degraded men—both natives and foreigners.

Having deprived her of this first right as a citizen, the elective franchise, thereby leaving her without representation in the halls of legislation, he has oppressed her on all sides.

The question of women's suffrage was highly contentious. Most men, including Stanton's husband, and many women were opposed to the idea. The issue was hotly debated at the Seneca Falls Convention. Frederick Douglas who famously said "if there is no struggle, there is no progress" attended the convention and argued in favor of adding the right for women to vote to the Declaration. Another attendee who added her voice to those in favor of granting women the right to vote was former First Lady, Dolley Madison, the widow of America's fourth President, James Madison, the man who wrote eleven of the Constitution's twenty-seven amendments.

The arguments for granting women the right to vote were compelling. Women pay taxes levied by men. Women obey laws made by men, and women suffer when politicians elected by men fail to do such basic things as stop untainted food from being sold. Women clean the homes, let them help elect politicians who will clean up the cities, counties, states, and the nation.

The arguments against giving women the right to vote were rooted in the presumption that women had neither the time nor the need to bother their pretty little heads with choosing political leaders. Opponents of women's suffrage claimed that women couldn't be bothered with voting. They were busy taking care of the home and children. They had to make the beds, cook the meals, do the dishes, wash the dirty clothes, and feed, bathe, and educate the children.

They didn't have the time to stay updated on politics. They didn't even need to be involved in them. A woman's Anti-Suffrage Association poster proclaimed that "the ballot will secure a woman no right that she needs and does not possess." Other posters showed men coming home after a hard day's work to a messy house because the women were too busy campaigning for the right to vote to attend to their duties. The message was clear. If women are given the right to vote, they will no longer be obedient housewives.

The New York State Association Opposed to Woman Suffrage circulated a poster showing a woman in a rocking chair holding a scroll with the words "The Ballot." The title of the poster was "Hugging a Delusion."

Elizabeth Cady Stanton and her followers were not deterred. In 1868, she and Susan B. Anthony started publishing a newspaper, *The Revolution*, that advocated for women's rights. They formed the National Woman Suffrage Association, which in 1890 merged with the American Woman Suffrage Association to create a unified movement under the banner of the National American Woman Suffrage Association.

Resistance to all male suffrage took many forms. In 1872, Susan B. Anthony voted in the presidential election. She was tried and convicted for illegally voting and fined $100. She refused to pay the fine. To avoid further publicity which would likely drum up support for giving women the right to vote, the authorities dropped the matter.

Other women also challenged laws that kept them from voting. Virginia Minor was prevented from registering to vote in St. Louis, Missouri. She filed suit, and in *Minor v Happersett* (1875), the Supreme Court in a unanimous decision ruled that citizenship did not confer the right to vote. Section 2 of the Fourteenth Amendment required that states not deny the right to vote to "male inhabitants...being twenty-one years of age, and citizens of the United States," but the Amendment didn't mention women. In the opinion for the Court, Chief Justice Morrison wrote:

For nearly ninety years, the people have acted upon the idea that the Constitution, when it conferred citizenship, did not necessarily confer the right of suffrage....Our province is to decide what the law is, not to declare what it should be.

We have given this case the careful consideration its importance demands. If the law is wrong, it ought to be changed; but the power for that is not with us. The arguments addressed to us bearing upon such a view of the subject may perhaps be sufficient to induce those having the power to make the alteration, but they ought not to be permitted to influence our judgment in determining the present rights of the parties now litigating before us. No argument as to woman's need of suffrage can be considered. We can only act upon her rights as they exist. It is not for us to look at the hardship of withholding. Our duty is at an end if we find it is within the power of a state to withhold.

In *Minor*, the Court tossed the women's suffrage ball back to the States. Each State could decide for itself if women were to be allowed to vote. It didn't happen overnight but with enough marches, posters, and national attention, slowly but surely, States started to vote on whether or not they wanted women's suffrage. Western states were more favorably disposed toward women's suffrage than those in the east. In 1890, when Wyoming was admitted to the union and became a state, the state constitution included the right of women to vote. By 1914, all of the western states had given women the right to vote.

It has been suggested that western states gave women the right to vote because they hoped that would serve as an incentive for women to move out west. The more likely explanation is that men on the frontier got to see firsthand how strong, resilient, and adaptable women can be. Frontier men had a great deal of respect for the women out there with them. Susan B. Anthony believed that the men out west were more chivalrous than those back east.

In the east, the push for women's suffrage continued unabated. The introduction of the automobile led to driving tours promoting the idea. One of the challenges the suffragettes faced was that the women's suffrage movement was linked to the women's temperance movement. Men feared that giving women the right to vote would lead to Prohibition. Susan B. Anthony believed that only by "putting the ballot into the hands of women" could the sale of liquor be banned.

A referendum on giving women the right to vote failed in New York in 1915, but was approved by the electorate two years later. In November 1917, when New Yorkers gave women the right to vote, the United States had been in the First World War for seven months. There weren't Rosie the Riveter posters, but women were contributing to the war effort.

An Amendment granting women the right to vote had, at the request of Susan B. Anthony and Elizabeth Cady Stanton, been introduced by a Republican Senator from California, Aaron A. Sargent, in 1878. Forty years later, on September 30, 1918, President Woodrow Wilson went to Capitol Hill and delivered a speech in the Senate chamber in support of women's suffrage.

> I regard the concurrence of the Senate in the constitutional amendment proposing the extension of the suffrage to women as vitally essential to the successful prosecution of the great war of humanity in which we are engaged. I have come to urge upon you the considerations which have led me to that conclusion.

On May 21, 1919, the Nineteenth Amendment was sent to the states. Carrie Chapman Catt, who in 1920 founded the League of Women Voters, led the effort for ratification. By the summer of 1920, thirty-five states had ratified the Amendment, but twelve had not. A newspaper article that praised the Virginia General Assembly for voting not to ratify the Amendment made it sound as if giving women the right to vote was unpatriotic:

> Every loyal American owes profound gratitude to the historic state of Virginia for upholding state's rights and federal

principles on which this government is founded and not giving women the vote.

In the end, it all came down to Tennessee where the Senate had voted to ratify the Amendment but the House was deadlocked. Harry T. Burn was a first-term Republican legislator. He had been convinced by senior members of his party to vote against ratification. But he received a letter from his mother urging him to vote for ratification:

> Hurrah and vote for Suffrage and don't keep them in doubt.... I've been watching to see how you stood but have not seen anything yet.... Don't forget to be a good boy and help Mrs. 'Thomas Catt' with her "Rats." Is she the one that put rat in ratification, Ha! No more from mama this time.

Burn changed his vote, and by a one-vote margin, the Tennessee House of Representatives voted to ratify the Nineteenth Amendment, and it became the law of the land. When criticized for voting to ratify the Amendment Burn said, "I knew that a mother's advice is always safest for a boy to follow, and my mother wanted me to vote for ratification."

Twenty-seven million women now had the right to vote, and on November 2, 1920, eight million of them exercised that right. H. L. Mencken wasn't thrilled with women's suffrage. He derisively wrote: "Without a doubt there are women who would vote intelligently. There are also men who knit socks beautifully." The Lebanese philosopher Charles Malek had a different view. He believed that "the fastest way to change society is to mobilize the women of the world."

And Carrie Chapman Catt had this message for the women of America:

> Now that we have the vote let us remember we are no longer petitioners. We are not wards of the nation, but free and equal citizens. Let us do our part to keep it a true and triumphant democracy.

The Twenty-Third Amendment: Voting Rights for DC Residents

The Twenty-Third Amendment gave the residents of the District of Columbia the right to vote in presidential elections. Ratified on March 29, 1961, it reads:

> The District constituting the seat of Government of the United States shall appoint in such manner as Congress may direct:
>
> A number of electors of President and Vice President equal to the whole number of Senators and Representatives in Congress to which the District would be entitled if it were a State, but in no event more than the least populous State; they shall be in addition to those appointed by the States, but they shall be considered, for the purposes of the election of President and Vice President, to be electors appointed by a State; and they shall meet in the District and perform such duties as provided by the twelfth article of amendment.
>
> The Congress shall have power to enforce this article by appropriate legislation.

The Constitution grants each state the number of electors equal to the total number of members of Congress (Senators plus Representatives) from that state. The District of Columbia is not a state. Article I, Section 8, Clause 17 of the Constitution gave Congress the power

> To exercise exclusive Legislation in all Cases whatsoever, over such District (not exceeding ten Miles square) as may, by Cession of particular States, and the Acceptance of Congress, become the Seat of Government of the United States

The Courts interpreted this Clause as giving Congress the power to govern the District of Columbia directly, or to allow it to be governed by officials elected by the District's population. The residents of the

District of Columbia had all the rights of residents of any of the states, except they had no Congressional representation, and could not vote in presidential elections.

Prior to moving to the new capitol city, Washington (in honor of George Washington), District of Columbia (in honor of Christopher Columbus), Congress had sat in eight different cities. The new seat of government was built on land ceded to the Federal Government by Maryland and Virginia. When Congress sat for the first time, on November 17, 1800, in the United States Capitol building, Washington, DC had a population of about 30,000.

The first attempt to grant District residents the right to vote in presidential elections was in 1888, but the amendment which was introduced by New Hampshire Senator Henry Blair was never sent to the states for ratification. Congress passed the Twenty-Third Amendment on June 16, 1960 in the midst of a presidential election campaign. Both party candidates (Richard Nixon and John F. Kennedy) endorsed the Amendment and nine months later it was ratified. The Amendment gives the District the same number of presidential electors as the least populous state, which as a practical matter limits the number of electors to three.

When the Twenty-Third Amendment was ratified in 1961, the population of Washington, DC had grown to over three-quarters of a million disenfranchised American citizens. The Twenty-Third Amendment gave them the right to vote in presidential elections, but they still had no congressional representation.

In 1970, Congress threw a bone to the District when it passed the District of Columbia Delegate Act. This granted residents of the District the right to elect one non-voting member to the House of Representatives.

In 1973, Congress passed the District of Columbia Home Rule Act. Its passage allowed the residents of the District to elect a mayor and a city council consisting of thirteen members. While in practice, Congress has given the mayor and council a pretty free hand in governing the city, it does still retain the power to review all proposed legislation. The House Committee on Oversight and Government Reform and the Senate Committee on the District of Columbia can modify or reject legislation enacted by the Council of the District of Columbia.

On August 22, 1978, Congress passed and sent to the states for ratification the District of Columbia Voting Rights Amendment. The proposed Amendment would have repealed the Twenty-Third Amendment and in its stead replaced it with the following: "For purposes of representation in the Congress, election of the President and Vice President, and article V of this Constitution, the District constituting the seat of government of the United States shall be treated as though it were a State."

Only sixteen states had ratified the District of Columbia Voting Rights Amendment by 1985 when the seven-year window for ratification closed. Opposition to the proposed Amendment was primarily based on the fact that by 1978, the residents of Washington, DC voted overwhelmingly for Democrats.

In the 1984 presidential election, Ronald Reagan carried every state except Minnesota, his opponent Walter Mondale's home state, and the District of Columbia. While the District's three electoral votes have never determined the outcome of a presidential election, adding Democrats to the House and Senate could tip the balance of power in those chambers.

Ratification of the District of Columbia Voting Rights Amendment would likely have guaranteed the Democratic Party two Senators and one Representative, or possibly even more than one depending on the District's population. For that reason, in the current political climate and for the foreseeable future, any attempt to resurrect the District of Columbia Voting Rights Amendment would be dead on arrival.

In 1846, Congress had returned to Virginia the land that it had ceded to form the District of Columbia. It has been suggested that one way to give the residents of the District the ability to vote in congressional elections would be to repeal the Twenty-Third Amendment and in its stead let District residents vote as if they were residents of the Maryland counties (Montgomery and Prince George's) bordering the District. That would require a constitutional amendment, but it would fully enfranchise the American citizens living in the District of Columbia.

The Twenty-Sixth Amendment: Old Enough to Fight for Your Country, Old Enough to Vote

The Twenty-Sixth Amendment lowered the voting age for all American citizens from twenty-one to eighteen. It was ratified on July 1, 1971, and reads:

> The right of citizens of the United States, who are eighteen years of age or older, to vote shall not be denied or abridged by the United States or by any State on account of age.
>
> The Congress shall have power to enforce this article by appropriate legislation.

In 1970, Congress passed amendments to the Voting Rights Act that lowered the voting age in federal and state elections from 21 to 18, banned states from using residency requirements to prevent people from voting in presidential elections, and made literacy tests illegal. A number of states felt that this was federal overreach, and that Congress had exceeded its constitutional authority.

In *Oregon v Mitchell* (1970), the Supreme Court in a 5–4 decision ruled that Congress had the authority to do all of the above with the exception of lowering the voting age from 21 to 18 in state and local elections. Justice Hugo Black, in the opinion for the Court wrote:

> The States have the power to set qualifications to vote in state and local elections, and the whole Constitution reserves that power to the States except as it has been curtailed by specific constitutional amendments. No amendment (including the Equal Protection Clause of the Fourteenth Amendment and the other Civil War Amendments) authorizes Congress' attempt to lower the voting age in state and local elections.

The Supreme Court handed down its decision on December 21, 1970. Congress quickly passed the Twenty-Sixth Amendment and sent it to the States for ratification three months later on March 23,

1971. It was ratified less than four months later on July 1, 1971, the shortest period of time for the ratification of a Constitutional Amendment.

In his 1954 State of the Union address, President Dwight D. Eisenhower had urged Congress to lower the voting age to eighteen. Before that, Eleanor Roosevelt had lobbied members of Congress to lower the voting age. During the Second World War, "old enough to fight, old enough to vote" was the rallying cry of those who supported lowering the voting age to eighteen. But many questioned whether an eighteen-year-old was mature enough to vote. They asked: Could eighteen-year-olds with their youthful spirit and lack of experience really be trusted with choosing our elected officials?

The Vietnam War changed that mindset. Eighteen-year-olds were being sent to fight in Southeast Asia. Didn't the young men who were being asked to fight, and perhaps die for their country, have the right to help select the men and women who were sending them to war? Eighteen- to twenty-year-olds accounted for far too many of the American deaths in Vietnam. The average age of the men killed in Vietnam was twenty-three.

The Senate report on the passage of the Twenty-Sixth Amendment answered Yes: "Younger citizens are fully mature enough to vote." Seems like that alone would do it. Especially because by the 1960s most Americans between eighteen and twenty-one had completed high school, and many had received at least some higher education. Second, the Senate report noted that eighteen-year-olds "bear all or most of an adult's responsibilities." Which is true, by the 1960s most eighteen-year-olds were either working or attending college or trade school. This consideration assumed special importance since anyone functioning as an adult in our society, whether paying taxes or fighting for our country, certainly deserved the right "to influence our society in a peaceful and constructive manner." If there is one thing America learned from the 1960s, it's that excluding people from the political process can lead to violent protests. After all Martin Luther King Jr. said, "Riot is the language of the unheard."

The Twenty-Sixth Amendment answered yes to the question if you are old enough to fight are you old enough to vote.

AFTERWORD

LOOKING BACK AND GOING FORWARD

Unratified Amendments

Of the twelve amendments that James Madison drafted, and Congress sent to the states for ratification on September 25, 1789, only one failed to be ratified. Which is for the best, since the Congressional Apportionment Amendment would have required that there be one member of the House of Representatives "for every fifty thousand persons." Today, with a U.S. population of 340 million, the 6,800 members of the House would need to hold their sessions in an arena. Eleven states did ratify the Amendment between 1789 and 1792, and theoretically it is still pending, but as a practical matter it will never see the light of day.

On May 1, 1810, Congress passed and sent to the states for ratification an amendment that would cause an American who accepted a foreign title without the consent of Congress to lose his or her citizenship:

> If any citizen of the United States shall accept, claim, receive or retain, any title of nobility or honour, or shall, without the consent of Congress, accept and retain any present, pension, office or emolument of any kind whatever, from any emperor, king, prince or foreign power, such person shall cease to be a citizen of the United States, and shall be incapable of holding any office of trust or profit under them, or either of them.

Congress did not set a time limit for the Title of Nobility Amendment, which was ratified by twelve states between 1810 and 1812. Theoretically, it is still pending.

On June 2, 1924, Congress passed and sent to the states the Child Labor Amendment, which if ratified would have given Congress the "power to limit, regulate, and prohibit the labor of persons under eighteen years of age." Twenty-eight states had ratified the Amendment by the end of January 1925. However, after the Supreme Court in *Darby*, which we discussed in Chapter 4, ruled that the 1938 Fair Labor Standards Act gave Congress the power to regulate conditions of employment for children under the age of 18, there was no longer an impetus for ratification. While no time limit was set for ratification, and theoretically it is still pending, as a practical matter, there is no longer a reason to ratify the Amendment.

On March 22, 1972, Congress passed and sent to the states, the Equal Rights Amendment. First proposed in 1923, the Amendment reads: "Equality of rights under the law shall not be denied or abridged by the United States or by any State on account of sex." Congress set a seven-year time limit for ratification. Prior to the 1979 deadline, thirty-five of the required thirty-eight states had ratified the Amendment but five of the states (Nebraska, Tennessee, Idaho, Kentucky, and South Dakota) that had previously ratified it, had rescinded their ratifications. Congress extended the deadline to 1982, but no additional states ratified the Amendment, so in 1982, it was generally accepted that the Amendment had failed to be ratified. In the years that followed, thanks in large measure to the efforts of Ruth Bader Ginsburg, the Equal Protection Clause of the Fourteenth Amendment has been used as the rationale for achieving the Equal Rights Amendment's goals.

On January 27, 2020, Virginia became the thirty-eighth state to ratify the Equal Rights Amendment, and shortly before leaving office, on January 17, 2025, President Biden issued a statement in which he affirmed that he believed that the Equal Rights Amendment had been ratified.

The American Bar Association (ABA) has recognized that the Equal Rights Amendment has cleared all necessary hurdles to be formally added to the Constitution as the 28th Amendment. I agree with the ABA and with leading legal constitutional scholars that the Equal Rights Amendment has become part of our Constitution.

The Constitution makes no mention of whether Congress has the authority to impose a deadline by which the states must have ratified a proposed amendment in order for it to become the law of the land. However, in *Dillon v Gloss* (1921), the Supreme Court unanimously ruled that Article V of the Constitution implied that Congress did have the authority to require that a proposed amendment be ratified within a certain time period. Writing for the Court Justice Willis Van Devanter stated:

> We conclude that the fair inference or implication from Article V is that the ratification must be within some reasonable time after the proposal. Of the power of Congress, keeping within reasonable limits, to fix a definite period for the ratification we entertain no doubt.

The Constitution also makes no mention of whether state legislatures have the right to rescind their ratifications. On July 20, 1868, Secretary of State William Seward informed Congress that as of July 9, the Fourteenth Amendment had been ratified. In his message to Congress, he noted that Ohio and New Jersey had since attempted to withdraw their ratifications of the Amendment. He concluded, "it is deemed a matter of doubt and uncertainty whether such resolutions are not irregular, invalid, and therefore ineffectual." Congress agreed and the following day passed a concurrent resolution stating that the Fourteenth Amendment had been ratified.

In *Coleman v Miller* (1939), the Supreme Court in a 7–2 decision concluded that it was up to Congress to determine if an amendment had been ratified. As Chief Justice Charles Evans Hughes explained:

> We think that...the question of the efficacy of ratifications by state legislatures, in the light of previous rejection or attempted withdrawal, should be regarded as a political question pertaining to the political departments, with the ultimate authority in the Congress in the exercise of its control over the promulgation of the adoption of the amendment.

Even if Congress decided that the actions of the five states that rescinded their ratification of the Equal Rights Amendment were invalid, because thirty-eight states had failed to ratify the Amendment prior to the deadline set by Congress, the Amendment will never see the light of day.

Proposed Amendments

Nearly 12,000 amendments have been proposed. Among them have been proposals to end birthright citizenship, require Congress to balance the budget, and limit the terms of members of Congress. None of the current proposals are likely to ever be passed by Congress and sent to the states for ratification.

On June 8, 2023, the Governor of California, Gavin Newsom, called for a Convention of the States to be assembled to consider proposed amendments to the Constitution, specifically one that he has proposed that would establish restrictions on gun ownership. While Article V of the Constitution provides that proposed amendments can be sent to the states for ratification by a Convention called by the Congress upon application by two-thirds of the State Legislatures, none has ever been called.

First, it would require thirty-four State Legislatures to vote in favor of holding a Convention, Second, there are no rules as to how a Convention would be conducted. Would Congress or would the

Convention delegates decide if each state was to have one vote, or would the number of votes each state had be proportional to that state's population? This is only one of the many contentious issues that would have to be addressed by Congress or the delegates to the Convention, and probably in the end by the Supreme Court.

Currently, there are four conservative groups lobbying for a Convention to be called. One wants a Convention to propose a Balanced Budget Amendment. A second group wants a Term Limits Amendment. The Wolf-PAC Political Action Committee wants a Convention to propose amendments that will "ensure balance, integrity, and transparency to our national system of campaign finance." The Convention of States Foundation wants a Convention to propose "amendments that will impose fiscal restraints on the federal government, limit its power and jurisdiction, and impose term limits on its officials and members of Congress."

The Convention of States Foundation gives the following answer to the why call a Convention question:

> Simple: to bring power back to the states and the people, where it belongs. Unelected bureaucrats in Washington, D.C. shouldn't be allowed to make sweeping decisions that impact millions of Americans. But right now, they do.

Liberal groups such as Common Cause oppose calling a Constitutional Convention. They believe a "convention is a dangerous and uncontrollable process that would put Americans' constitutional rights up for grabs." Common Cause points out that while each of the groups calling for a Convention have pledged that the delegates to the Constitution would be restricted to only proposing amendments that their group has advocated for, the Constitution doesn't provide any guidance, "there are **absolutely no rules**."

> That means the group of people convening to rewrite our Constitution could be totally unelected and unaccountable. There is nothing that could limit the convention to a single

issue, so the delegates could write amendments that revoke any of our most cherished rights—like our right to peaceful protest, our freedom of religion, or our right to privacy. There are also no rules preventing corporations from pouring money into the convention to ensure they get their way.

In short, an Article V Convention would be a disaster. It would lead to long and costly legal battles, uncertainty about how our democracy functions, and likely economic instability.

Twenty-Eight State Legislatures, for one reason or another, have voted in favor of calling a Constitutional Convention. But given today's political realities, the chances that one will be called are slight, and even if one were called, any amendments proposed by the delegates to the Convention would still require ratification by thirty-eight states.

The Framers recognized that making changes to the Nation's Founding Document was not a matter to be taken lightly. They wanted to be certain that when changes were made, they had the support of Congress and the States. The assent of two-thirds of the members of both the House of Representatives and the Senate, and three-quarters of the State Legislatures is required to amend the Constitution. The twenty-seven amendments that have been ratified are a testament to their foresight. From 1791, when the first ten amendments (The Bill of Rights) were ratified until 1992, when the Twenty-Seventh (the Congressional Compensation) Amendment became the law of the land, the amendments have played, and will continue to play, a vital role in our continuing efforts to form a more perfect union.